W9-CDH-264

TURNING

30

TURNING
30

How to Get the Life You Really Want

Sheila Panchal & Ellen Jackson

Marlowe & Company
New York

TURNING 30: *How to Get the Life You Really Want*
Copyright © 2005 by Sheila Panchal & Ellen Jackson

Published by
Marlowe & Company
An Imprint of Avalon Publishing Group Incorporated
245 West 17th Street • 11th Floor
New York, NY 10011-5300

AVALON
publishing group incorporated

This book was published in somewhat different form in the United Kingdom
in 2005 by Piatkus Books. This edition was published in 2006 by arrangement
with Piatkus Books.

Library of Congress Cataloging-in-Publication Data

Pancha, Sheila.
  Turning 30: how to get the life you really want / Sheila Panchal & Ellen Jackson.
      p. cm.
  Originally published: London: Piatkus Books, 2005.
  Includes bibliographical references.
  ISBN 1-56924-310-7
    1. Career changes—Decision making. 2. Career changes—Case studies. 3. Job
satisfaction—Case studies. I. Title: Turning thirty. II. Jackson, Ellen, 1972– III.
Title.

  HF5384.P36 2006
  650.1—dc22

                                                              2005054427

  ISBN-13: 978-1-56924-310-7

  9 8 7 6 5 4 3 2 1

Designed by Goldust Design
Printed in the United States of America

CONTENTS

THANK YOU

To all of you who have shared your thoughts, ideas, enthusiasm, experience, and Turning 30 stories and have helped us to write this book. You know who you are, and we couldn't have done it without you.

Special thanks from Ellen go to Jenny, Barry, Lucy and Nigel, Veronica, Michelle, George, Robert, and Peter. Sheila sends extra love and thanks to Gemma, Brigid, Jane, Edith, Susie, Sarah, Vikki, Emma, Poppy, Rachel, Helen, Lisa, Bunny, Simon, Dan, James, Lawrence, Annette, Merlin, Sam, Abbey, Claire, Susan, Caroline, the Diamond Club, and to her wonderful parents. And especially to Gel, my love—this book is for you.

We would also like to thank everyone at the Coaching Psychology Unit of the University of Sydney for their teaching and leadership, as well as our past and present colleagues for their help and inspiration. Thanks also to Jonny Pegg at Curtis Brown for his belief, enthusiasm, and support, and to Alice at Piatkus for her excellent advice.

ABOUT US

Ellen's story

Ellen was 27 years old, sitting in her office, staring out of the window and imagining her future. She knew she wanted financial independence and freedom from tedious "How was your weekend?" conversations in the office break room. She knew she needed to escape corporate life and make her own way. But how? Where was she going to find real career satisfaction, and how was she going to make it happen?

These were Ellen's first thoughts as she grappled with the lead up to 30. Then she took some tentative steps toward a new life. She quit her corporate job and went back to study to become a registered psychologist. She moved into a home office and employed her own office assistant, Oscar (the Persian cat).

Since then, as a self-employed consultant psychologist, Ellen has helped people on either side of 30 to make positive changes to their lives. She has trained as a coaching psychologist and has particular expertise in career change, based at least in part on her own experience.

Sheila's story

At 26, Sheila found herself increasingly fed up with how life was turning out—too much work, too few choices, and not enough fun. Added to this, she knew deep down that she didn't buy into the promotion games at work and couldn't see a future at the management consultancy she worked for. It just didn't add up anymore.

Convinced there was more to life than a laptop and microwave dinners, she suffered a true turning-30 panic and decided to make some big life changes. She swapped London for Sydney, and meetings for flower-arranging classes! Suddenly her corporate job was a thing of the past and she had the chance to start again. It was time for some soul searching and a great deal of hard work.

By the time she returned to London, she had struggled through her Turning 30 Blues and found renewed enthusiasm for life. She cofounded Happiness First, a company that helps people and organizations put happiness first. She still owns a laptop.

An idea was born

We were training at the University of Sydney's Coaching Psychology Unit when we met for coffee to discuss a newsletter or something. Hours later we were deep in conversation about the trials of turning 30: the career crises, the love laments, the changing relationships with family and friends, and the challenges of finding a life that works.

We realized that most people we knew were looking for ways to deal with a distinct life wobble in the lead up to 30.

We discussed what we thought was happening: our own experiences; those of friends, clients, and colleagues; and our different techniques for helping people through. By the time we left that coffee shop we were on a mission. Our goal: to write a book for people grappling with turning 30, sharing our knowledge and experience as psychologists and fellow survivors. This is it. We hope you like it.

YOU KNOW YOU'RE TURNING 30 WHEN . . .

You find that suddenly the world's full of cute babies that you simply must stop to coo at.

You listen to NPR exclusively.

You love nothing better than a night in, watching interior design and cooking programs.

You have absolutely no clue what's no. 1 in the charts.

You are obsessed with property.

You say things that sound horribly like things your parents would say.

You find that arranging a night out is a month-long nightmare experience.

You get more excited about a roast on Sunday than a night out clubbing.

You stop dreaming of becoming a professional baseball player and start dreaming of having a son who might.

You try to outdo your friends in a "who can throw the best dinner party" competition.

You become powerless to resist the lure of self-assembly furniture.

You always have enough milk.

You realize you left school a long, long time ago.

Instead of complaining about old people who take ages to get off the bus, you complain about schoolchildren who use bad language.

You worry about your parents' health.

You become envious of other people's hanging baskets.

You come face to face with the realization that you are but passing through this life . . . And if you don't settle down and have kids soon, it might be too late . . . And you really ought to be doing something with your life . . . And you're destroying millions of brain cells every time a quick drink turns into a big night out . . . And look at that—a full set of nonstick saucepans and you get an omelet pan thrown in . . .

INTRODUCTION

You may not be ready to admit it, but you're no longer 21. The big 3-0 is approaching and life isn't turning out as you'd planned. You're not a super-successful, mega-rich, globetrotting entrepreneur with an ultramodern city apartment, sports car, designer clothes, and entourage of beautiful people. You're not even a semi-successful, financially secure professional with your own two-bedroom condo, a permanent relationship, and a busy, satisfying social life.

If you're turning 30 and you know there must be more to life than a dreary job, a lackluster love life, an oversupply of obligations, and an undersupply of play, then this is the book for you. In it we examine the "I really don't know what I'm doing with my life" syndrome that so often hits as your 30th birthday approaches. We call it the "Turning 30 Blues." Chapter by chapter we explore the issues you're struggling with as the odometer of life clicks over to your 30s. How do you find a career you love and a love life you can't live without? How can you juggle your commitments to friends and family so that you can spend more time with who you want when you want and still have time for yourself? Just what is work/life balance anyway? And how do you keep in shape, physically and emotionally, and still make sure that you're getting the absolute maximum out of life?

We've written this book to help you solve the dilemmas that descend as life gets a little bit more serious and you get a little bit more serious about it. In each chapter we have included exercises, tips, facts, and ideas that will help you to sort out your career, your love life, your relationship with family and friends, and your health and well-being. We'll guide you through the process of setting and achieving goals in each area of your life and give you the lowdown on finding happiness in all its shapes and forms.

But most importantly, we're going to help you find out who you are and what you really want out of life, because once you know yourself, getting what you want becomes much simpler.

Approaching 30 is a tumultuous time. A lot can change, but all times of change open doors to new possibilities. It's all about getting the life you really want.

Which Turning 30 Type are you?

Type	What you do	What you say
Must-be-married	You're convinced life will be perfect once you've found your happily-ever-after	I'm looking for my future husband/ wife.
Got-to-keep clubbing	You're not about to let go of your 20s. You're out every Thursday, Friday, and Saturday night—as well as a few mid-week.	That's the third night this week I've been home at 5 a.m.
Career-obsessed	You're hell-bent on reaching the top of that career ladder and have been known to sleep (alone) at the office.	I must impress the boss.
Bridget-Jones-all -over-again	You're fed up with single life, flirt with anything with a pulse, and secretly frequent speed-dating nights.	So, are you a Virgo?
Forever-21	The last ten years have passed you by. You're certain you've just left college and you're still not planning any- thing beyond your next meal.	Kraft maraconi and cheese for dinner again tonight?

Do-it-yourself kings and queens	You spend all your weekends in DIY shops and own at least one power tool.	Have you seen the new range of almost-white emulsions from Sherwin-Williams?
Must-go-traveling	You're gearing up for your next backpacking trip even though you know you can no longer live without a hairdryer.	So, tell me about Venice.

How to use this book

This is a "doing" book. It is designed not only to get you thinking about the challenges of turning 30 but also to get you doing things that will help you through the ups and downs and move you closer to the life you really want.

In chapter 1 you get a better idea of what's behind your Turning 30 Blues. We introduce you to the Pizza of Life, our way of helping you make sense of your vague feelings of unhappiness and confusion. Each pizza slice focuses on a different life area—work, love, friends and family, and health and lifestyle. You get the chance to review where you are now with each of the four slices and to work out how you really want life to be as you head toward 30.

In chapter 2 you build on this picture to create a profile of who you are—your values, your strengths, and your personal style. This profile will help you to fill in the gaps in your understanding of yourself and to make the right decisions about your future. Then in chapters 3 to 6 we return to the pizza to explore each area of your life in more depth. We talk about the dilemmas that people face when they're turning 30 and help you set goals and take action to get your career, love life, relationships with your family and friends, and health and lifestyle in top shape. In chapter 7 you reflect on happiness, and by the end of the book we hope that your Turning 30 Blues will be a thing of the past.

Tips for success

1. Take notes!

While you're reading each chapter, spend some time thinking about what you are reading and the impact on your life, and take notes! We have included plenty of space for notes as you go along. These don't need to be long or even insightful, but you should jot down any thoughts as they come to mind—maybe things from plans you had in the past or points that might be useful to you in the future. The important thing is that you write them down. This not only forces you to stop and think, but it also gives you a record of your ideas that you can work from as you make changes in the coming days, weeks, months, and years. It's likely that you will come back to your notes many times over and build on them further. You'll also be able to look back at where you started your journey, and as you make progress you can congratulate yourself on how far you have come.

2. Do the exercises!

There are many exercises throughout the book that we use with clients and that we'll introduce you to as you explore your life and your goals for the future. Here's a tip—do them! They are included for a reason. Each exercise is designed to help you think more carefully about the information you have read and to allow you to work out how to use it in your own life. If you do the exercises, you are much more likely to have one of those "Aha!" experiences that make all the difference between reading something interesting and learning something that will change your life.

3. Believe in yourself!

You only have one life, and it's up to you to make the most of it. When you're making changes, have patience and give yourself the time to think about what's going on. Find quiet, calm spaces to sit and think. Change doesn't happen overnight, but every small step takes you forward. By picking up this book you have taken the first step toward working your way through your Turning 30 Blues and making the most of life in your 30s. It might be a difficult journey at times, but it's absolutely a journey worth taking. It's a journey toward finding purpose and contentment. Remember to keep an open mind, be honest with yourself, and most of all—enjoy every step of the way!

CHAPTER 1

The Turning 30 Blues

Remember when you were 20 and life was simple? Straightforward? You danced till dawn, drank past closing time, and dated people you knew you shouldn't. You worked hard, played hard, spent money on stuff you didn't need, and didn't worry about wrinkles or responsibilities. At 20 you had your whole life ahead of you. You were the young one, the up-and-comer, the kid with the world at your feet. You gave no thought to the future or what it would hold. At 20 you lived life for the moment. Your future was just where you'd live out your dreams, and back then it was still a long, long way off.

Now you're turning 30 and life is a little more complicated. You might not be weighed down by much more than a job, a lease, and friends who enter and exit between business trips, but time is passing and you're beginning to become aware of it.

Maybe you're starting to wonder about how you can turn your run of dreary, pays-the-bills jobs into a focused, fulfilling career. Or perhaps you're thinking that it's time to rethink your "bikini models only" dating strategy and begin the search for someone with whom you might be able to share your future. Your parents might be hassling you to ditch the backpack and settle down, while you may be hoping that the answer to your questions is waiting for you in the plains of Africa. Or you may be seriously doubting your decision to become an accountant but don't feel able to face starting over and pursuing your filmmaking dream. You may be tired of working like a demon and wondering whether to stop chasing the big bucks and get a social life (or any life) instead. You may even feel just plain restless.

*"Life was ticking along quite nicely in my 20s. There were a few ups and downs, but nothing major. When I turned 30, I literally went crazy for about a year. It was a nightmare. Everything was fine on the outside: I had a great job in publishing, lovely friends I had known for years, but I just started to hate it all and feel unsettled about my life in general. I felt annoyed that I had reached this stage and had nothing to show for it. It was a really strange feeling, and I just couldn't shake it." **Laura, 31***

Approaching 30 you're often reconsidering, contemplating,

and wondering. Life may feel unsettled, a little strange. You may be more reflective, more uncertain than you once were. Where are you now? What do you really want from life? Have you made the right decisions? Have they worked out the way you thought they would? What have you achieved? Is it really what you wanted? Are you really who you thought you were? What are your plans now? Are you on the right path? And if not, how do you find it?

It's all about growing up

If you're turning 30, feeling anxious and uncertain and searching for the path to a more contented life, the first thing you need to know is that you're not alone. In fact, between the ages of 28 and 32 most of us can expect to experience more change, uncertainty, and angst than we have since our teenage years.

Why?

During your late 20s and early 30s you go through a kind of emotional growth spurt, an intense period of figuring out what life is all about and where yours is heading. Other experts call it the Age 30 Transition. We call it the Turning 30 Blues. It doesn't get the PR spin of puberty blues or the midlife crisis, but it's a legitimate upheaval—like teenage angst without the tantrums.

The Turning 30 Blues are an important milestone in the process of growing up. At 18 you may have thought you were a fully formed adult ready to take on the world, but usually at that age you have only just begun to understand who you are and how you operate. At 18 you may have been independent for the first time—you washed your own clothes and rustled up a grilled-cheese sandwich for dinner—but you probably hadn't really thought about who you wanted to be as a person or what you wanted to achieve in your life. Let's face it, at 18 your plans for the future probably didn't extend much beyond the next weekend.

Most people enter the next phase of development at 22 or thereabouts and stay there until they are 27 or so. During these years you may have formed more serious relationships, and if you went to college or grad school you will have finally finished studying and started your working life. By this stage you may have begun to give some thought to what you want from life, but it usually isn't something you take too seriously. You may have focused your attention on one particular area—your career or your relationship with your partner—or you might have traveled the world or dedicated your life to soccer, music, or ballroom dancing. For the most part, though, you have simply been having fun socializing, spending money, working hard, and partying hard. Life usually doesn't put too much pressure on you to be grown up and responsible at this stage, and if you do think of the future, it is just to dream of all the brilliant things you will do one day.

Cue the Turning 30 Blues

We don't really know what it is that turns you from a

blissful 20-something into an angst-ridden almost-30. It might be the prospect of your 30th birthday—that big neon-lit reminder that you're getting older and that life won't last for ever. Some experts speculate that it hits when you realize that the decisions you made about life in your early 20s—about your work, family, friends, lifestyle, money, and ideals—don't fit you anymore. These decisions will have been made when you knew less about the world than you do now and even less about yourself. Now, as life changes around you, you're having to reassess those decisions and think about what your life will look like in the future. It's no wonder that you can start to feel that you want to make changes.

The Turning 30 Blues

"I was really starting to think that I was having some kind of breakdown. Everything had been cruising along nicely— my job, my girlfriend, golf on Saturday, and the bars on Saturday night . . . It was cool. Then, I don't know what happened, but I was just angry all the time. I was a real pain, particularly to my girlfriend, but I couldn't stop it. I just wasn't happy with anything anymore. My job really annoyed me, and I started dreading Monday morn- ings. I'd never been like that before. I mean, work was never a joy, but I was happy enough. I'd never wanted to leave. Then all of a sudden I couldn't stand the place. I wanted to pack everything in and start my life all over again

somewhere else. I didn't even get a buzz on the golf course anymore." Chris, 31

The Turning 30 Blues can be pretty tough. They can creep up on you gradually—you feel vague dissatisfaction and frustration with your life, but you can't pinpoint what needs to change for you to feel better—or they can hit you head-on, as an immediate sense of crisis. One minute everything is rolling along nicely, and then the next you hate your job, your relationship is suffocating, everything about your lifestyle is plainly wrong, and you're thinking of running off to start all over again in Brazil.

So what are the symptoms of the Turning 30 Blues? And what can you do to get over them and get on with your life? Let's take a look.

Getting to know yourself

Throughout this book we talk about the importance of getting to know yourself in order to live a happy and satisfied life. In fact, in the next chapter we will help you uncover your strengths, your values, and your personal style. That way you can be sure that the decisions you are making and the goals you are setting are truly right for you.

But when dealing with your Turning 30 Blues it's also useful to have a good understanding of what's going on now and why. So, as you read the next section, think about what you're going through as you turn 30. Why are you asking questions, considering your future, or contemplating your past? What are you discovering that will help you through your Turning 30 Blues? Find a piece of paper and make notes as you read. You might be surprised at what you learn about yourself.

1. You're asking questions

What am I going to do with my life? What's my destiny? Am I going to end up alone, broke, in a crummy job? Can I marry out of my religion? Will I ever be happy with how I look? Will my parents be around when I have children? Am I with the right person? Is it too late to do the things I want? Do I go out enough? Do I go out too much? Am I getting boring? Should I be successful by now? Will I ever want children? What's the point of all this? Will anything exciting ever happen again? Who am I anyway?

The Turning 30 Blues is all about questions—lots of them. You won't know the answers to most of them. You *can't* know the answers to some of them—at least not yet. Will your parents be around when you have children? Who knows? As for "Should you be successful by now?"—well, what is success anyway? That's another question.

Asking a lot of questions and not knowing the answers can be very unsettling, because we like certainty in our lives. But if you're going to grow as a person, you can't avoid asking questions of yourself. At some time you have to start reflecting, otherwise you run the risk of having fun day to day but never getting it together and fulfilling your potential.

Exercise: Your questions

What are the burning questions that you need answered? Make a list of your questions below and put them in priority order.

My Turning 30 Questions

_____

_____

_____

_____

_____

_____

_____

_____

_____

_____

_____

_____

_____

_____

Now take a look at your list. Are all of your questions really about you, or are you making plans for your friends and other people around you? Do you want to settle down and have children, or is that what your family wants you to do? Are you looking for career success or just following the path of others? Are you doing something—anything—not because it makes you happy but because of an ill-defined feeling that you "should"?

The confusion of the Turning 30 Blues is often made worse when you compare yourself to other people (and you always do). You look at your friends and others your age and see their successes (never their struggles) and wonder whether you are keeping up. Instead of getting comfortable with what's right for you, you get caught up in looking for outside evidence that you have made the right decisions.

When you are thinking about the issues you are facing, your hopes for the future, and the goals you are setting, always make sure that you are considering what's right for *you*, what *you* want, not what you think you *should* be doing or what you think you *need* to do to keep up with those around you. It's not always easy to shake off outside pressures, but if you focus on who you really are and what you really want out of life, then you'll increase your chances of making the right decisions and will be much happier as a result.

2. You're thinking about the future

There's a first time for everything, and the Turning 30 Blues is often the first time that people start to think seriously about their future. It's as if a "responsibility switch" gets flicked and all of a sudden you start to wonder whether you want marriage, career, children, financial security, a home of your own . . .

In your 20s fantazising about the future may have been a favorite pastime. You may have whiled away many happy hours thinking about the exciting, glamorous life you would soon be living. As 30 approaches, though, reality kicks in. Now you're likely to be thinking less about a fantasy future and more about the cold, hard facts of where you are today. It may occur to you that if you're going to achieve what you want to in life, you're going to have to start work right now.

"You spend your 20s waiting for the world to fall in your lap. You think that an amazing career and sexy boyfriend will turn up somehow, sometime. We expect stuff like that just to happen. As you approach 30 you realize for the first time that it isn't going to and you need to do something about it. You realize that you have to become an active agent in your own life." Jo, 32

This realization that you might have to do something about your life can come as a result of the decisions and actions of those around you. If you have friends who are getting married or moving overseas, you might start to think about whether these are ambitions you have, too. But it's not just external influences that change the way you feel. You also get an inward sense that time is passing and that you need to set some goals and start making things happen now.

Exercise: A Perfect Future

In our work with clients we see over and over again the power of imagining the future. By creating an image of what you want your future to look like, you get a better sense of your true goals, hopes, and aims. Then, by writing these down, you get a little closer to making them reality.

"Whatever your dreams are, go for them, no matter how much you doubt whether you will succeed. At least you won't spend the rest of your life wondering 'What if?'"
Kim, 27

TRY THIS:
Find a place where you feel comfortable and relaxed. Now free your imagination and pick a date in the future, somewhere between three and five years' time. Imagine exactly what your ideal life looks like on that day and start writing about it in the space provided, as though you are writing a letter from your future self to your present self. Describe how you are living each day, who you are with, what your world looks and feels like. Be as specific as possible. Where are you working (if you're working)? Where do you live? What does your home look like? How are you spending your free time? Who is in

your life? How do you feel? Be expansive and creative, and don't hold back.

As you do this, consider the following questions:

What would I do if I knew I couldn't fail?

What would I do if I had the guts to do it?

What would I do if I had unlimited freedom?

Who is living the life I most envy? What do I think it's like?

What would I do if I were ten times bolder?

My Perfect Future

_____

_____

_____

_____

_____

_____

_____

_____

_____

_____

_____

_____

_____

_____

_____

_____

When you've finished, reread your letter and think for a few minutes about what you've written. Are you already on the path to achieving what you see in your future, or are there changes that you need to make? Make some notes about what you've learned and then keep reading. We'll come back to your vision of a perfect future when you're ready to set some goals.

3. You're reflecting on the past

*"In my early 20s I did whatever I wanted. I didn't feel any pressure to settle down to a career and a steady home life. I loved my life and happily traveled and 'bummed around.' In my late 20s I have begun to feel guilty about not using my education and perhaps fulfilling some of my potential. I'm a bit anxious about getting older, not having used my degree, not having a high-powered job, not saving for my future and settling down." **Lee, 29**

You can't consider your future without giving some thought to your past. After all, it's your past that has brought you to where you are now, and whether that's a good or a bad thing you need to be reconciled to it before you can move on. If turning 30 is prompting you to ponder what the future holds, it's logical that you will reflect on the decisions you have made so far in order to figure out whether they have provided you with a sound base from which to launch yourself into that future.

So what has happened so far? Are you doing what you want to be doing work-wise? Have you lived and loved in your past relationships in the way you want to in the future? Do you have the kind of bonds with your family and friends that you would like to have? Are your current lifestyle and financial situation setting you on the path to reach your goals for the future? The answers to these questions can be confronting, particularly if after many years of study and commitment you're starting to wonder whether beekeeping really is the career for you, or if you've got an inkling that a life of boozing and partying isn't such a great idea after all, but that's all you seem to have done so far. It's all too easy to sink into a reverie of regrets and might-have-beens.

What you've done in the past and what you expect for the future can be very different, and sometimes you can feel torn between the two. When both seem attractive but in different ways, it's a tough one.

"It feels like a toss-up between thrills and stability. The 'thrills' lifestyle involves lots of going out, spending money on frivolous things, drinking too much, and generally being irresponsible and decadent. The 'stable' lifestyle looks like a house and garden, barbecues, and days out in the country. Both are appealing, so we get stuck in this situation where we don't know what we really want. Maybe a life of barbecues with friends plus some low-grade drugs would be a good compromise!" Simon, 26

If you don't feel that your life is what it could be on the cusp of 30, this is your chance to amp things up and to make the changes you need. The Turning 30 Blues might be unsettling, but they bring with them the opportunity to think back over the decisions you have made in your life so far and to plan how you're going to change things, starting today, to make sure you are heading for a great future. The past may have been brilliant, but now's your chance to make the future even better.

Life changes

When we work with clients we talk about the "Pizza of Life." We look at the four key areas of your life at 30, each of which is represented by a slice of the pizza. Big changes can take place in each slice during the Turning 30 Blues. It's up to you to decide.

> *"The things I am concerned with are finding a home, feeling that I have got somewhere to settle, finding work that is challenging and that makes me want to get up every day, and finding someone I want to grow old with. This makes quite a change from thinking about where to go on vacation, whether to buy those amazing pink shoes in* Vogue *and being late for work."* **Angela, 27**

We've dedicated a chapter to each pizza slice later in the book, but let's take a quick peek at what you can expect as 30 approaches . . .

Slice 1: Earning a living

Turning 30 is a prime time for career crises. Not only are you reflecting on the career choices you have (or haven't) made so far, but the need to think more carefully about your future can propel you into contemplating a career change. You might decide that it's time to make more money, to settle on a serious career path, or to finally follow your heart and find a job that's in the field you've always longed to work in.

Slice 2: Love life

The Turning 30 Blues can be a tough time for relationships, with many a partnership falling by the wayside as people reassess their lives and decide what they want for the future. If you got married or settled into a permanent relationship during your early or mid-20s, you might find that you both feel the strain as one (or both) of you takes stock. But it's not all bad news. If the two of you can survive this kind of upheaval and keep the relationship intact, you're destined to emerge stronger and the relationship will be better for it.

Slice 3: Nearest & dearest

Subtle changes can take place at 30 when it comes to your friends and family. After years of hovering in the background, your parents (and siblings) may edge a little further into your awareness. You may become suddenly conscious of their health and find yourself factoring their needs into your decisions. Your friends, on the other hand, may be coupling up and moving away. You still love them to death, but you need to find new ways to stay in touch.

Slice 4: Leisure, pleasure & healthy living

As you turn 30 you will probably realize that pizza and beer are no longer a sustainable diet and that you can't avoid some form of exercise if you want to stay in shape. It's often also time for a lifestyle shift as you swap all-night clubbing for dinner dates and succumb to the lure of the latte.

Exercise: The Pizza of Life

Many of our clients come to us with a vague but unsettling feeling that things aren't quite right. They know they're not happy with the way life is, and they're ready to make some changes, but they haven't quite been able to pinpoint what it is that needs to change.

The Pizza of Life exercise helps you to take a look at each area of your life and turn these vague feelings of unhappiness and confusion into specific goals.

Here's what you need to do:
Step 1: For each of the four life pizza slices, make a quick assessment of your level of contentment and give it a rating out of 10, where 1 = "Complete misery, this area of

---

my life is a total disaster" and 10 = "Fantastic, I wouldn't be happier with this area of my life if I got to spend every moment of it with Brad Pitt/Angelina Jolie."

Clearly there are other life areas that are important, such as finances and physical environment, but we have only included those areas that are likely to be trouble spots during the Turning 30 Blues. Feel free to add others if you like.

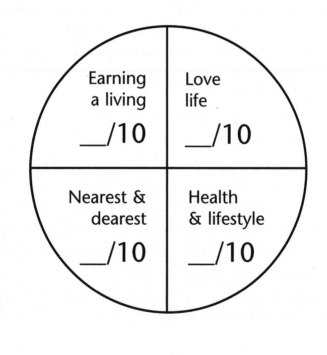

Earning a living __/10

Love life __/10

Nearest & dearest __/10

Health & lifestyle __/10

How did you do? Which area of your life looks healthiest? Which needs emergency treatment right now?

Step 2: Now that you have a rough idea of where you are with each of your pizza slices, make a list for each slice of five things that you think you need to do to get that rating closer to 10. For example, if you've given your career a rating of 6 out of 10, what would make it a 7 or 8? Do you need to change jobs? Find a career you're happy with? Be paid more money? Kill your boss? (Note: We're not advocating murder, work-related or otherwise.)

Tip for success: Think back to your "Perfect Future" letter, and use it to think about what sort of things you need to be doing in each area of your life. What's going to get you that little bit closer to your dream?

The things I need to do to improve my pizza ratings:

Earning a living	Love life
1.	1.
2.	2.
3.	3.
4.	4.
5.	5.

Nearest & dearest	Health & lifestyle
1.	1.
2.	2.
3.	3.
4.	4.
5.	5.

You are now on your way to shaping the goals that will help you overcome your Turning 30 Blues and enjoy a great 30-something life. In the next chapter you'll learn more about setting goals and how to make them happen. We'll also come back to these goals in chapters 3–6 and give you the chance to explore them further.

Astrology's take: Saturn's Return

Psychologists are not the only ones to notice that something unsettling happens to us when we hit 30. Astrologers have long talked about Saturn's Return— the period between the ages of 28 and 32 in which we reassess our choices. They believe that when we reach 30(ish), Saturn, the taskmaster or teaching planet, returns to the same position in our horoscope as it was at the time of our birth, triggering a period of self-evaluation. These are testing times when we make serious decisions that add to our maturity and wisdom. Astrologers believe that you don't really grow up until you have experienced Saturn's Return.

What else can you expect when you turn 30?

So far we have talked about the internal changes that you go through in your late 20s and early 30s that lead to the questions, the angst, and the reflection of the Turning 30 Blues. But it's not just what's going on inside you that makes things complicated. It's also what's going on around you.

Social changes

The world is a vastly more complex, demanding, and engulfing place than it was when your parents were your age. Revolutions in communications technology have given you 24/7 TV channels that address every interest, and spam e-mail offering you everything from penis extensions to maps of celebrity homes; in vitro fertilization enables first-time motherhood at 50; competition at work increases all the time as wage differentials between high and low earners widen; cut-rate airfares and globalization allow you to live and work overseas almost as easily as if you were commuting to the next town.

Today you get to decide what job you'll do, who you'll go out with (or marry, or sleep with, and when), what you'll wear, where in the world you will live, when you'll travel, which car you'll buy, and whether or not you'll have kids. You can also choose which religion you'll be, whether to dye your hair blue, what to call yourself, and how much money you'll spend on your cell phone, massages, music, and MasterCard.

Life is more exciting, inviting, and full of possibilities than it has ever been before. But with this choice comes complexity. You have the freedom to do it all your way, but you have the responsibility to get it right.

"There's a huge responsibility in realizing that, ultimately, you are the one responsible for your own life—the choices you make, the people you choose to be around, the job you have, all of that. But there's an even bigger freedom in that."
Lucy, 27

All in all, it's hard to see this kind of freedom as a bad thing. Certainly most of us have no desire to go back to the days when you were expected to stay in a bad marriage or stick with an unsuitable career. But there is a downside that makes the decisions you're facing during the Turning 30 Blues a little bit more challenging. As you are faced with more and more choice, it gets harder and harder to figure out which is the right decision for *you*.

This is when "choice anxiety" hits—that push–pull feeling that you get when you know there are lots of paths you can take, but you don't know which is the *best* one to follow. Unfortunately, when we're faced with endless options, we don't tend to assess the situation calmly and make the choice that best suits our needs and aspirations. It's never as easy as that. Instead, we get stuck looking for the best decision among a million options. Rather than take advantage of the possibilities the world is presenting us with, we tend to get so bogged down looking for the right answer that we stay where we are, feeling frustrated and a little sorry for ourselves.

Great expectations

Added to this is the pressure caused by expectations—
your own expectations, those of others, those of society
itself. Do you meet the expectations of the "perfect"
30-something?

☐ I'm a successful, professional something-or-other, and I
boss at least three people around.

☐ I've found my life partner, and we live in perfect
domestic bliss.

☐ I've slept with at least 15 people (including at least one
Italian millionaire or one French waitress).

☐ I go on regular mini-vacations to exciting destinations.

☐ I have a great apartment and an even better sofa.

☐ I own a blender, juicer, all the Emeril Lagasse cook-
books, and a set of "good knives."

☐ I've got clever/sensible financial arrangements like
retirement plans.

☐ I've leapt from a plane, done a bungee jump, or
engaged in some other thrilling and potentially life-
threatening activity.

☐ I've stopped acting like a 16-year-old with my parents.

☐ I've got great hair.

☐ I live near all my friends and we get along great. It's like
the set of *Friends*.

☐ I've got two well-behaved and incredibly cute kids (or at least know what I'm going to call them).

☐ I regularly see my personal trainer, who is also a celebrity body coach.

How many did you check off? How close are you to being the "perfect" person who's done everything they "should" have by 30? And does any of it matter?

Clearly none of it does matter, but it's hard to rid yourself of the feeling that maybe, just maybe, it does and you're falling dismally short of where you should be by now.

And if the choices spread before you are already causing you stress, the pressure you can feel from the expectations of parents, friends, the media (and yourself) can be enough to send you right over the edge. Your mom might be on you to "find someone nice," while your dad's worried about your financial security. Your best friend thinks you should build bridges in Africa with her, and your colleague at work is convinced that the two of you should start a cake-making business. On top of that, the magazine you read on the subway says you should consume only 38 calories a day and exercise 12 times a week. It also informs you that the average celebrity is ten years younger than you yet earns over 100 times as much. The TV advises you that with the aid of some cosmetic enhancement, a new Fendi handbag, the latest model Porsche, or a whopping great loan, you too can be happier, prettier, more popular, and just a better person all around.

Some expectations are fair. It's probably not unreasonable for your parents to expect you to be washing your own clothes and paying your own cell phone bill by the time you're 30. But other expectations create pressure to do more, be more, have more, and spend more than you need. Society tells us that money equals success and success equals happiness. This adds to the sense that you need to get on top of things, get things right, and get moving before you get left behind.

This conviction that we have to "have it all" leaves us working harder, playing harder, filling every spare minute with activity, and feeling as though we're on a treadmill that we can't get off. We can work hard for our next promotion and pay raise and sacrifice life for cash that we don't have time to spend and enjoy. In fact, research shows that even though every indicator of wealth has increased over the past fifty years, rates of clinical depression have soared. The link between wealth and happiness appears to be nothing more than an urban myth.

Exercise: Keeping it simple

If the multitude of choices is bringing you turning-30 confusion and the pressure of expectations is leaving you feeling jaded, there's a simple thing you can do to relieve the burden—get it out of your head and onto paper.

TRY THIS
Choices
Step 1: Make a list of the top five choices that you are

facing in your life right now. They might be choices about your job, your relationships, your finances, your lifestyle, or anything else. Write them down here.

The choices I have to make:

1. _____
2. _____
3. _____
4. _____
5. _____
6. _____
7. _____
8. _____

Step 2: For each choice you are facing list as many alternative courses of action as you can possibly think of. Brainstorm. Include even the utterly ridiculous. Write them all down below.

My options:

1. _____
2. _____
3. _____
4. _____
5. _____
6. _____
7. _____
8. _____

Now look back at your list and cross out all of the options that you would never seriously consider and those that might be okay but don't really push your buttons. How many are left?

Does your decision seem a little simpler now?

Expectations

Step 1: List the major influences in your life. These might include your parents, other relatives, friends, current partners, ex-partners, colleagues, and bosses.

My influences:

1. _____
2. _____
3. _____
4. _____
5. _____
6. _____
7. _____
8. _____

Step 2: Next, think about their expectations of you. What do they want or expect you to do with your life? Do your parents expect you to get a good job, marry a nice local girl or boy, and produce grandchildren? Do your friends expect you to spend each night hanging out in cocktail bars and never getting any sleep? Does your boss expect you to charge up the career ladder? Make a note of others' expectations below.

Their expectations of me:

1. _____

2. _____

3. _____

4. _____

5. _____

6. _____

7. _____

8. _____

Step 3: Take a look at what you have written. How realistic are these expectations? How contradictory are they? Most importantly, are they in line with what you want to achieve in life?

Now is your chance to decide to which (if any) of these expectations you subscribe. If there are some that match your own goals in life, then make a note of them and we'll explore them further when you start setting goals later. If others don't match your needs, ditch them. This is your life and yours alone. It's important to respect others' opinions, but you can't live your life according to their wishes. You don't need the extra pressure.

Your next steps

Congratulations! You have taken the first step toward over-coming your Turning 30 Blues, and you're on your way to getting the life you really want. The Turning 30 Blues may be troublesome and a little frustrating and confusing at times, but on the positive side, this is the beginning of an exciting new phase of your life. You can finally leave the insecurities of your teens and 20s behind you and look forward to a new decade in which you will live a happy and fulfilled life.

Your next step is to find out a little more about yourself—to uncover the values and beliefs you hold dear, learn more about your strengths and abilities, and discover your unique personal style.

CHAPTER 2
Making Changes

Did you know?

Happy, successful people:

✦ Think carefully about what they want from life and find a way to make it happen.

✦ Have goals, plans, and ambitions (sometimes in simple, subtle ways).

✦ Know what makes them special and unique and how to use that uniqueness to best advantage.

✦ Are willing to work hard to get what they want.

✦ Are willing to ask others for help and support.

✦ Are willing to take a chance.

✦ Know that we get what we give and that happiness is a choice and a state of mind.

When was the last time you sat down and really thought about who you are, what's important to you, and what you want from life? Have you ever done it? If you have, is it clear in your own head?

We rarely sit and assess where we are in life. Who's got the time when there's work to do, meals to cook, and friends to see? In the whirlwind of daily life it's easy to let life fly by. We fight the little battles—sorting out problems at work and dealing with the ups and downs of relationships—but we tend to let the big things like our hopes, dreams, plans, and ambitions slide by, hoping that they will somehow take care of themselves.

Making the time to figure out who you are is a vital step in overcoming your Turning 30 Blues and realizing those dreams.

"I feel that I got lost in my 20s. I spent all of my time running away from the pressure of expectation and chased a hedonistic lifestyle of drugs, drink, and socializing. I guess I realized that it couldn't go on forever. I needed to face up to my responsibilities, and that meant I had to get to know

myself again, to establish a sense of myself as an adult. I asked myself a lot of questions. Was I the same person I was when I left college? Did I want the same things? They're tough questions, but I knew that until I answered them I wouldn't get anywhere." **Anthony, 29**

Establishing who you are—with all your unique skills, talents, and wisdom – allows you to do four important things:

1. Make the right decisions and choices for you (rather than simply following the expectations of your best friend, your parents, your partner, or your neighbor's dog).

2. Confidently navigate your way through all the options and possibilities out there.

3. Develop greater belief in your abilities, your strengths, and all of the special things that you bring to the world and gain a much stronger sense of self. This will allow you to accept and value who you are rather than wishing you were more like your dad, girlfriend, or Tom Cruise.

4. Build the basis for a happy and successful 30-something life.

There are two main areas to explore in this chapter. The first is "Getting to Know Yourself." This is when you ask yourself "Who am I at 30?" or thereabouts. What are the key things you need to know about yourself in order to live life the way you really want to live it?

The second is "Making It Happen." This walks you through a four-step process for making changes in your life.

So, first of all, who are you? What's important to you?

Your values

....

Your values are your beliefs about the important things in life. They are your principles, the standards that you use to guide yourself through life and stop yourself living at the whim of accidents, habits, impulses, and emotions.

Being fully aware of your values makes turning-30 decision-making a more straightforward exercise. If you know that independence is important to you, you're able to make decisions about your work, your relationships, and your lifestyle that allow you to be independent. If you value self-expression, you can make choices that give you the chance to express yourself.

Living according to your values feels comfortable, reassuring, and right. On the other hand, living in conflict with them can leave you feeling uncertain or uncomfortable.

Exercise: What's important to you?

If you've never really thought about what's important to you, here's your chance to find out.

Step 1: Take a look at this list of values, and circle those that strike a chord in you. If you are having trouble, the following questions may help:

What are you passionate about?

What inspires you?

What do you admire and look for in others?

What sort of situations, behavior and qualities do you avoid in yourself and others?

Achievement	Helping society/others
Acknowledgment	Honesty
Adaptability	Humor
Artistry	Imagination
Authenticity	Independence
Beauty and aesthetics	Influencing others
Being admired	Integrity
Being alone	Intellectual stimulation
Being different	Interaction
Being valued	Intimacy
Being with others	Joy
Belonging	Love
Change and variety	Making decisions
Collaboration	Meaning and fulfillment
Communication	Meeting challenges
Community	Money
Competition	Order
Comradeship	Participation
Control over time	Peace
Creativity	Personal empowerment
Excitement	Physical health
Expanding knowledge	Power and authority
Freedom to choose	Profit
Friendship	Recognition
Fun and enjoyment	Respect

Security	Stability
Self-determination	Status
Self-expression	Success
Self-fulfillment	Support
Sensuality	Time
Sexuality	Tranquility
Solitude	Zest
Spirituality	

Step 2: Think of three specific examples of ways in which you are living according to your values. Maybe you have an interest that allows you to be creative, or your work gives you great intellectual stimulation. When you are living by your values, it is likely to feel genuine and "right." Write your three examples below.

1. _____

2. _____

3. _____

Step 3: Think of three values that are important to you that you are not using (or not using enough) in your life right now. What would you like to be doing that would allow you to live by these values? Write your ideas below.

1. _____

2. _____

3. _____

Your strengths

If we asked you to list the three things that you are best at, what would they be? Are you brilliant at solving problems or coming up with creative ideas? Are you a whiz at mending, speaking in public, or cooking great Thai food? You may find this difficult, as we're so much better at noticing what we're not good at than what we are—not surprising, given the fact that we will have been criticized over 250,000 times by the age of 18 and praised only 30,000 times!

Your strengths are the skills that you are good at and enjoy using, and they play an important part in your turning-30 decisions. Identifying your strengths gives you extra insight into the choices facing you. What's more, you get a stronger sense of your contribution to your workplace, your family, your community, and your world, and that's great for your confidence and self-esteem.

Some strengths appear very specific and not necessarily that useful. You might have an encyclopedic knowledge of car models, for example, or a knack with broken toasters. This might be handy if you're having a toaster crisis or need to impress car-loving friends, but it might not be instantly obvious how these skills are going to make life easier as you turn 30.

What's important to remember is that every minor skill is evidence of your broader, more significant strengths. If you can name the make, model, and production year of every vehicle that crosses your path, you probably have a good memory for detailed information. If you can fix a broken toaster, you may have a talent for mechanics.

Knowing your strengths means that decisions about what you should do with your life become easier. Playing to your strengths means living a more successful, satisfied life.

Exercise: Uncovering your strengths

Step 1: Make a list of the activities that you enjoy and that you think you're good at under each of the following headings.

Physical/Manual	Intellectual	Social/Relationships

Step 2: Quite often those close to us can see our strengths better than we can see them ourselves. Ask your friends and family what they believe your greatest strengths to be and write their answers in the space below.

My strengths (according to my nearest and dearest):

_____

_____

_____

_____

_____

_____

_____

_____

_____

_____

_____

_____

_____

_____

_____

_____

_____

_____

_____

_____

Your style

Your personal style, or personality, is the third and final piece of this "Who am I at 30?" puzzle. Your personal style is the way that you prefer to behave or operate. It is the set of characteristics that, in combination, make you do what you do, need what you need, love what you love, and be who you are. Your personal style affects everything you do and the way that you do it, and understanding it makes your actions, your decisions, and your life more comprehensible.

Think for a minute. When you're out with a group of friends, do you take center stage and dance on tables, or do you get yourself a drink, stand back, and quietly take in the scene? When you're making a decision, do you carefully weigh the pros and cons, or do you make a quick assessment based on what feels right? When you're completing a piece of work, do you persevere until it's perfect, or do you stop when it's good enough and move on to something else? These characteristics are all aspects of your personal style.

If you are behaving in a way that's consistent with your personal style, you're comfortable. If you have to act in a way that's not consistent with your personal style, whether at work, in your relationship, or in some other area of your life, you may feel awkward. You can do it, but it's harder work. It doesn't flow as well as behaving in line with your own personal style.

When we're growing up, peer pressure reigns and we hate to admit that we're in any way different from anyone else.

If we're not into the same things as the cool kids, we pretend that we are. Later, we try out different jobs, relationships, friends, locations, and so forth and notice that some experiences feel great and others don't. These feelings are great signals. They tell us about what does and doesn't work for us. Yet we often ignore them and instead feel inadequate about not fitting in. If everyone around us seems to enjoy talking about politics or listening to techno or getting stoned, we feel that we should as well and tell ourselves that we should try harder. Instead of being ourselves, we end up wishing we were more like other people.

It's important to remember that there is no ideal personal style. It's not better to be outgoing than quiet, or practical than creative. Each characteristic has its pros and cons. The point is to understand and accept yourself and live life in a way that works for you.

Knowing your personal style, like knowing your values and your strengths, helps you to make the right decisions during the Turning 30 Blues. If you can find the perfect match between who you are and how you live your life, you're destined for a fulfilling future.

Exercise: Moment of fame

To get an insight into your personal style, imagine someone is making a TV documentary about you. In that documentary your best friend is asked to describe your personal style. Which five words would he or she use to describe you? Take a look at the list below if you need help. If you're not sure, be brave and ask!

My personal style:

1. _____

2. _____

3. _____

4. _____

5. _____

Achieving	Decisive
Adaptable	Detail-minded
Analytical	Dutiful
Apprehensive	Emotional
Attached to the familiar	Experimental
Caring	Flexible
Cautious	Forward-thinking
Competitive	Imaginative
Confident	Impatient
Conscientious	Impractical
Controlling	Indecisive
Conventional	Independent
Cooperative	Innovative

Intellectual	Private
Intuitive	Quiet
Lively	Rational
Logical	Relaxed
Modest	Restrained
Nonconforming	Skeptical
Objective	Self-assured
Open	Self-reliant
Open to change	Sensitive
Optimistic	Serious
Organized	Shy
Outgoing	Sociable
Outspoken	Solitary
Persuasive	Steady
Pessimistic	Tough-minded
Practical	Trusting

Summary point

By now you will have completed a number of exercises designed to help you work out who you are, where you are, and what you want. Here's your chance to reflect on what you've learned so far.

Exercise: Reflection time

My questions: What are the three big questions I'm asking myself during the Turning 30 Blues?

1. _____

2. _____

3. _____

My Perfect Future: What are the three most important things in my Perfect Future?

1. _____

2. _____

3. _____

Here and now: What do you need to do in each area of your life to move toward that Perfect Future?

Career	Love life

Family & friends	Health & lifestyle

My choices: What are the three most important choices I am facing in my life right now?

1. _____

2. _____

3. _____

My expectations: What do I (realistically) expect of myself at this time of my life? What expectations do others have of me that I choose to live up to?

1. _____

2. _____

3. _____

Who I am at 30: What are my values, strengths, and personal style at this point in my life? (Remember to keep

these in mind when considering decisions and changes, as
they will help you to do the right things for you.)

Values	Strengths	Personal style
1.	1.	1.
2.	2.	2.
3.	3.	3.
4.	4.	4.
5.	5.	5.

Making it happen

Exercises like the Pizza of Life and the Perfect Future letter
are the first step in building a broad picture of how you
would like your life to be. Knowing who you are—your
strengths, your values, and your personal style—allows you
to fill in some of the detail and be more confident that the
plans you are making are the right ones for you personally.
But there is something else you need to know if you're
going to emerge successfully from the Turning 30 Blues and
get the life you really want—and that's how to make
changes and how to make them stick. Making changes, even
small ones, can be scary. Follow these steps to make it easier.

Step 1: Setting goals
The first thing you need to do if you're going to make
your perfect dream a perfect reality is to set some specific

realistic goals. A broad picture of what you want to achieve in life is great for motivation and inspiration, but it doesn't get you from here to there.

That's where goals come in. Goals are a mechanism for making change happen. They're vital because they tell you exactly what you want, what you're going to do, and how you're going to do it. Good goals even tell you when you're going to take each step.

It's important that goals are written down in black and white. In 1979, students from Harvard were asked whether they had clear written goals that they wanted to achieve after they graduated. Of all the students, 3 percent had written goals, 13 percent had unwritten goals, and 84 percent had no goals. Ten years later, the 3 percent with the written goals were earning, or worth, ten times as much as the other 97 percent. That should motivate you to write it all down!

Before you rush to get a pen and paper, though, you need to look in a little more detail at how to go about setting your goals. Make sure that you're making them SMARTER.

Specific It's no good setting yourself a goal to "Be happier" or to "Have a successful career." They're not goals, they're just wishes. A really specific goal should give you some idea of the steps you need to take in order to achieve it. For example, instead of "I will explore some new career options," say "I will research five new career options in the next two weeks on the Internet."

Measurable When you're working toward a goal, it is important for your motivation that you are able to rate your progress. People normally measure themselves just on outcome, but that's not always the full picture. For example, you could have a goal of losing six pounds in two weeks. Success measures here could be "Being six pounds lighter and feeling more confident." If after two weeks you've only lost three pounds but you feel great, then you certainly haven't failed.

Attractive Does your goal excite you? Are you raring to get started? If your goal doesn't interest you, it's unlikely you're going to put forth the effort to make it happen.

Relevant Is the goal in line with your Perfect Future, values, strengths, and personal style? Ask yourself:
✦ Does my goal keep me moving toward

where I want to be?

✦ Does my goal fit with my values, strengths, and personal style?

✦ Does this goal feel right to me—does it come from my heart?

Time-bound Without a realistic deadline, you'll drift on and on. There's nothing like a deadline to get you motivated!

Effort Reality-testing your goals is critical—don't set yourself up for failure by giving yourself an unrealistic goal. Do you really think you can manage to earn a million dollars in the next month? The chance of that lottery win is pretty slim. Set yourself goals that are within reach. There is nothing more demoralizing than feeling that you have to give up everything for your goal. If you're too ambitious, you'll get discouraged, and if you're too easy on yourself, you won't be stretched.

Reward This is the thing that everyone forgets, but it's the most important! It's easy to focus on what we haven't done rather than what we have. So celebrate the little successes as well as the big ones. What's your reward for what you've done this week? What's your reward for reaching your goal? A weekend away? An afternoon reading in the sun? Lots of chocolate?

Step 2: Baby steps

Once you have set your goals, you need to work out how you're going to reach them, and that means action planning.

The key to an effective action plan is to keep it simple. It's often tempting when you're excited about your goals and the amazing impact they are going to have on your life to take on too much too quickly, but this only increases the chances of it all going horribly wrong. On the path to achieving goals it's often slow and steady that wins the race. The best way to keep yourself on an even keel is to break your goal down into tiny, tiny baby steps and take at least one step every day.

At the end of the next four chapters you will have the chance to take a look at your goals in detail and make a note of all the steps you need to take to reach them. You will write brief plans that start right away and finish when you have achieved your goal. You will need to be realistic about the time frame and note down the milestones that you have to reach during that time. If you're planning a career change, do you need to update your resumé? If so, do you need to find it? Once your resumé is ready, are you planning to see a career coach or a recruiter? If you write down each and every step that you need to take and plan to take a step every day, you'll be amazed how quickly you move forward!

Step 3: Staying motivated

How many times have you set yourself a goal, gotten really enthusiastic about it, thrown yourself in at the deep end, lasted three or four days at best, fallen in a heap, and gone back to your old ways? Once? Twice? A thousand times? Going to the gym springs to mind!

Achieving your goals is all about changing your habits, and anyone who has ever tried (unsuccessfully) to quit smoking, get fit, or lose weight (and that's most of us) can tell you that changing your habits is hard work.

The good news is that there are some simple things that you can do to keep yourself on track. Try these:

Make a case for change

It's always easier to make a change if we really know why we're doing it. So, for each goal that you set yourself as you read this book, ask yourself:

+ What is the biggest benefit for me in achieving this goal?

+ How will I feel in a year from now if I do nothing about achieving this goal?

✦ What do I have working in my favor that will help me achieve this goal?

Write your answers on a piece of paper and pin them up somewhere you will see them every day. That way you will have a constant reminder of what you are achieving and why.

Keep track of your progress

Keep a diary or journal of the steps that you are taking toward your goals each day. Make a note of each task that you are committed to doing, and once you have done it, mark it off with a big check. This is a great way to see the progress that you are making each day and to keep yourself motivated!

Ask for help

There's nothing like telling someone else about your goals to keep you committed, particularly if you know that that person will be supportive and enthusiastic. Tell someone you trust. Explain the sort of support you would like from them. There are other sources of help available, too. Personal trainers, coaches, psychologists, trainers, professional associations, and community groups can all help in different ways. Find something that works for you.

Step 4: Getting back on track

When things are going well, working toward goals is an exhilarating experience, but what do you do when the wheels come off and your best-laid plans go awry? Obstacles are inevitable when making any change, and while you will successfully overcome most of them, there will be an odd one that throws you off track.

If this happens, the first thing to remember is that your worth is not defined just by this one task or goal. Also, relapse is a very normal part of making any change in your life, and if you do find yourself slipping into old habits, it's not a reason to give up! Setbacks are only temporary and certainly not the end of the world.

If you have trouble on the path to achieving your turning-30 goals, try the following:

✦ **Acknowledge your relapse and figure out what has caused it.** If what you're doing isn't working, try something different. There are many solutions to every problem. So you're on the Atkins diet and you can't resist a doughnut in the office one day? You could see this as failure and give up. Or you might decide to change your boundaries and allow yourself two doughnuts a week.

✦ **Don't dwell on it.** Life doesn't always go according to plan, and happy, successful people (and that's you) take note of what's not working, learn from it, and keep going. They don't just focus on results—they enjoy every step along the way. The most important thing is to stay positive and believe in yourself. That will get you a long way.

Now you're all set to make the changes that are going to lift you out of your Turning 30 Blues and toward your exciting future. The next chapters look at the areas of your Pizza of Life in more depth. They review the main dilemmas people face in each area, looking at why they are happening and offering ideas for moving forward. This is your chance to explore your questions, choices, and changes in more detail, and at the end of each chapter you will be in a position to set goals for that particular area of your life.

Good luck!

CHAPTER 3

Earning a Living

Quick Quiz: Is your career in crisis?

Choose the statements that describe you:

✦ I dread Monday mornings.

✦ I always feel stressed at work.

✦ I really love the people I work with, but I'm bored with my job.

✦ I'm irritable all the time.

✦ I feel underappreciated.

- ✦ I have never really enjoyed what I do.

- ✦ I long for weekends and vacations when I can forget about work.

- ✦ I really want to change my career, but I don't know how.

- ✦ I used to love my job, but I've lost interest recently.

- ✦ I enjoy my job, but I'm not making the best of myself.

- ✦ I work too much. I need to find some balance in my life.

- ✦ I can't believe I still haven't found a career I'm happy with!

How many did you check? One? More than one? Many more than one? If you're overworked, overstressed, or just over your job, you're not alone. In fact if you're turning 30 and not having a career crisis, you're the odd one out. According to research, only one in three of us feel we have found real fulfillment at work on the eve of our 30th birthdays. The rest of us reckon we've chosen the wrong path, can't find a job we enjoy, are torn between our sensible, I'm-doing-the-right-thing job and the career of our dreams, or are just ready to pack it all in and move to the countryside.

Mark's story

Mark started work as a dentist right after dental school. He joined a local practice and worked hard. He liked his clients and he liked his boss—and for the first couple of years he liked his work. It wasn't always so cool probing around in people's mouths, but it was great to be out doing what he was trained to do, and he was always learning something new. But a few years into his great career Mark started feeling lost. He wondered whether he really wanted to be a dentist for the rest of his life. He found it harder and harder to get enthusiastic about his work and eventually took a year out to travel. He hoped that once he'd had a break he would rediscover his enthusiasm for his job. No such luck. When he returned from his trip, he couldn't face going back to dentistry. He took a couple of casual jobs and spent a lot of time hanging out with his friends. He tormented himself with what he called his "failed career." He wished he could go back in time to choose a different educational course and take a different path.

Mark's story might be familiar. How many people do you know who feel they've made the wrong career choice or are still looking for work they can get passionate about? How many people do you know who are bored at work? Or who work too hard? Or who still haven't got their "career" together at all?

It's normal these days to have two or more careers in a lifetime, so if you're having a career dilemma, don't let the "job for life" mentality stop you from making changes. In the following pages we look at the top turning-30 "Career Crises" and what you can do to conquer them. You'll discover more about what causes career angst in your late 20s and early 30s, and you'll work out your career goals for a successful 30-something life.

Career Crisis 1: Help! I hate my job!

One of the biggest career upsets you can face at 30 is coming to grips with the fact that after committing years of your life to studying or training and working your way up the career ladder, you no longer enjoy what you do. In fact, if you're honest with yourself, you may never have enjoyed it! You might have lived for years with the sneaking suspicion that you made entirely the wrong career choice. You became a doctor when you should have been a designer, or you took up law when your heart was in landscape gardening.

It's very easy to wander along the wrong career path and not realize until it's (seemingly) too late. You are so young when you start out. In your teens you don't know enough about yourself to choose a suitable haircut, let alone a career that you'll enjoy for the next ten, twenty, or thirty years. You're influenced by your parents' expectations, their hopes and dreams for you, your exam results, your friends' choices, and (God forbid) your well-meaning school counselor, who thinks accountancy is the perfect career for everyone.

"I never wanted to be an engineer, but I did well at math and science so my parents and teachers thought it made sense. Today I'm six years down the track and I hate it. What do I do now?" **Chris, 28**

Until now you've done the "right" thing and persevered with engineering, dentistry, banking, or beekeeping, because you put the time and energy into learning the ropes and it's a good job. It makes your parents happy, it's stable, the pay is good, and, let's face it, you're not qualified to do anything else. But now you're pushing 30 and you're bored, frustrated, and disillusioned. You think there must be something else out there that really pushes your buttons. You want desperately to make a switch—but to what? How do you find the right job for you?

Working out what you really want to do with the rest of your life is tough. It takes time and it takes commitment. If you're like most of us, you've picked up the newspaper after a particularly demanding week, scanned the job ads, felt depressed, and decided that a career change is just too hard—like getting fit or finding the perfect pair of jeans. But while finding a job you love is difficult, it isn't impossible.

Finding a career that you really love is all about learning more about yourself. It's like putting together the pieces of a jigsaw puzzle to reveal a picture of who you are, what you're good at, what you love and hate about work, and what you need from a job in order to be truly satisfied.

Exercise: Your career jigsaw

If you're suffering from a turning-30 Career Crisis, here's your chance to get clear on what you want in a job and why!

Step 1: Your dream jobs

If we asked you to tell us which jobs you didn't want to do, you'd list them in an instant: "Accounting is too boring, social work is too depressing, stockbroking too stressful, garbology too, well, smelly." But have you ever sat down and written a list of the jobs you *would* like to do? Try it now. List five jobs you'd love to do. Let your imagination run wild. Don't worry about the practical aspects of your choices, like whether you've got the right qualifications or could survive on the salary. Just list five or six jobs that really capture your imagination. What did you write in your Perfect Future letter?

My top five jobs are:

1. _____
2. _____
3. _____
4. _____
5. _____

What do these jobs say about you? Are there any themes or patterns? Think back to your values, strengths, and personal style.

Step 2: Your skills and knowledge

Your dream jobs tell you about the areas in which you might like to work, but you also need to know what skills and knowledge you have that will help you make changes.

List the skills and knowledge that you have acquired over the years. Have you learned to drive a forklift truck or diagnose an illness? Do you know the ins and outs of speechwriting for politicians or how to produce a newsletter? Have a look at your strengths from chapter 2. Think long and hard, and come up with as long a list as you can.

Next, whittle your list down to your top five. Which do you enjoy most? Which are you best at?

My top five skills and knowledge areas are:

1. _____

2. _____

3. _____

4. _____

5. _____

Step 3: Likes and dislikes

Now it's time to learn from your experience. Make a list of all the tasks you have loved in previous jobs and all the tasks you haven't enjoyed. Have you enjoyed creative tasks such as building things or problem solving? Do you avoid process-oriented tasks such as meetings or filing reports?

To create your inventory of likes and dislikes, give five answers to each of the following questions:

From all my past work and personal experiences, what have I loved doing?

From all my past work and personal experiences, what have I really not enjoyed?

Likes	Dislikes
1.	1.
2.	2.
3.	3.
4.	4.
5.	5.

Step 4: Who, what, when, where and how

Make a note of your answers to the following questions.

Think about the job you have enjoyed the most. What was your work environment like? Did you work in a team or on your own? Was it competitive or collaborative? Was it fast-paced or easy-going? Did you have a lot of say in what you did and how you did it, or was your work structured by someone else?

✦ Do you want to work full-time or part-time, in a big office, a factory, a store, or from home?

✦ Do you want to be self-employed?

✦ What sort of people do you like to work with? What are they interested in? What are they like to be with?

✦ Where would you like to work? Near home? In the city?

✦ How much money do you need to earn?

✦ What other benefits would you like? A company car? Extra vacation time?

Step 5: Putting the pieces together

Now it's time to put the pieces of your puzzle together and get started on working out your perfect career path. Settle yourself on the sofa and take a look at what you've written down so far. What have you learned about yourself? Has this exercise given you any ideas about possible careers? Has it triggered any memories of jobs you once considered but never pursued? If someone asked you to list your top five possible career options based on what you have learned about yourself, what would they be? (Tip: Think about fields—areas of work such as travel, medicine, finance—as well as roles—specific jobs such as administrator, producer, consultant.) Get creative and write them down here.

My possible career options:

_____

_____

_____

_____

_____

_____

My possible career options (cont.):

_____

_____

_____

_____

_____

_____

_____

_____

_____

_____

_____

_____

_____

_____

_____

_____

_____

_____

_____

_____

_____

_____

_____

Now that you've completed your career jigsaw, it's time to build on what you've learned so far.

1. **Research.** Start researching your career options. Invest some time and energy and find out more about each one. What does a typical day look like? What qualifications and training are required? Find out as much as you can from contacts you may have, the Internet, calling companies, and talking to people. Write down everything you learn.

2. **Make some choices.** Once you feel you have enough information, it's time to make some decisions. Which of these options appeals most? Which do you think might be worth pursuing? Choose one or two and get started.

3. **Take action!** This is where the traditional job search comes into play. Once you know what you're looking for, it's time to go and find it. Newspapers, Internet job sites, contacts, and networking are all ways of chasing that job. Look back at what you learned about goal setting in chapter 2. Set SMARTER goals, make an action plan, and make time each day to do something about pursuing your dream career, however small. Stay positive, learn from obstacles, and hang in there—you're on the path to a career you'll love.

Finding your purpose in life

We often talk about finding a purpose in life—that job or career that's going to make us feel complete, that we have a reason to be here on Earth. Of course your purpose may have more to do with your family and friends than your career. But here are some tips that will help you find it.

Tip 1. Be patient. Finding your purpose in life takes time. It's not a problem to be conquered in a day or so, but a learning process that involves trial and error.

Tip 2. Think of every job as a stepping-stone on your journey. Use each new job as an opportunity to learn more about yourself and to piece together the jigsaw puzzle that will, piece by piece, reveal your purpose.

Tip 3. Treat every job as an adventure. If you approach your job with the attitude that you're there to learn as much as you can, you'll not only enjoy it more, but you could also be amazed at where you end up.

Career Crisis 2: I've found my perfect career, but I'm too scared to give it a try!

What happens if you know exactly what you want to do with your life but you're not sure if you're ready to take that leap into the great unknown? It's a tough call. You've put in long hours to get to where you are in your current job, and the investment is paying off. You're finally receiving recognition for your skills and expertise, or you're being paid well for your hard work. You've developed a lifestyle to suit your income, and you've made friends with your colleagues. You want to follow the dream, quit your job, and start work on your novel, but you know it's not that easy. How will you pay the rent for a start?

In your 20s you tend to live with the dream and get on with reality, but as you get older and think more about the future, you realize that there is only so much of your life left, and you find yourself thinking more and more about your long-held plans to work for a charity or to make your living as a writer. What was once just an item on the list of things to do "one day" becomes an increasingly more tempting option.

Joe's story

Joe is the production manager for a furniture-making business. He's been in the job for five years. The pace is frantic, and he has his share of problems—staff who don't turn up, unreliable suppliers, a grumpy boss. Joe joined the company because he's passionate about furniture. He's harbored a secret dream of starting his own furniture business for years, but he hasn't yet had the courage to give it a try. There's always a reason why now is not the right time—he's just been given a promotion, bought a new car, blown all his money on a surfing trip . . . As the days go by, Joe agonizes over his "should I stay or should I go" dilemma. He fights a constant internal battle, second-guessing himself and doubting his own judgment about which path to follow. One day he's full of optimism: "I know I can do it. I just need to get started." The next he's not so sure: "Maybe I'm not cut out to run my own business. Maybe it's too hard. Maybe it's not realistic. Maybe I'm delusional."

Making a major change in your life is a scary thing to do, whether it's moving abroad, ending a relationship, starting a business, or changing career. You might gain a lot, but you'll probably lose something, too, and it's usually the thought of what you'll lose that stops you from getting on with it. Joe is experiencing all of those feelings. He really wants to start his business, but at the same time he knows there are risks involved. He could lose money, he'll certainly have to survive on a lower income at first, there will be a lot of hard work involved, and there's a chance that he won't succeed, that reality won't live up to his dreams.

This kind of ambivalence is completely normal. It's part of the cycle of thoughts that we all go through when we're contemplating a change. Do I or don't I? Should I or shouldn't I? Eventually, though, you can't keep going around and around in circles like that. It's exhausting. Ultimately, you have to make a decision—is it time to take the leap or not?

Exercise: Overcoming your fears

If you're dreaming of making a new start, whether it's a job change, a career change, or a new business venture, but you're feeling frustrated and uncertain, try this exercise. In the left-hand column below list every possible reason you have for leaving things as they are and not changing anything. Why should you stay in your current job and not take the leap?

Then, make a list in the second column of every possible reason for making the change. Make sure you think of the immediate reasons, like staying sane, as well as the long-term reasons, like your ultimate financial position or the benefits for your home life.

Reasons not to change	Reasons to change

> Once you have your two lists, take a look at the result. Do you, deep down, find one set of answers more convincing than the other? Are your answers (and your gut feelings) telling you that you're ready to make a change? If so, what's the first baby step? What small thing can you do today to get you started on your new path? How can you move forward in a way that doesn't seem scary or extreme?

Career Crisis 3: Work is taking over my life!

You've probably noticed that working hours are getting crazier by the year. Research has found that over 90 percent of us do some of our weekly work outside regular working hours, and over half of us work on weekends. The proportion of full-timers working more than 40 hours per week has risen from around one-third to just under half. In fact, today more than three-quarters of workers say they'd gladly trade some of their income for more flexibility, allowing them to work and have a personal life.

As a late 20- or early 30-something, you're probably one of those people who are lamenting the loss of your personal life due to work commitments. Finding a balance between work and play has become the Holy Grail for our generation. We're determined not to commit every waking moment of the next forty years to our work in the same way our parents did. We want to spend time with friends, to travel, to chill out, and to enjoy life. We're keen to swing the pendulum away from the "work comes first" mentality and back toward a life that allows us to work and spend time the way we want to spend it. We might still be working like crazy, but we're determined to get the balance right—someday.

"It happened so slowly that I didn't notice anything day to day, but work was taking over my life. I found myself being too busy to accept invitations from friends, getting annoyed at phone calls, not having the time to go to the gym or the supermarket. It felt as if the rest of my life was crumbling away beneath me, while my job was consuming increasing amounts of time and energy. I knew something was wrong when I realized my friends had stopped calling me and when I did see them the only thing I could think to talk about was work—BORING!" **Susan, 27**

Like many of life's challenges, finding a balance between your work life and the rest of your life can be difficult. In many workplaces there's an unspoken competition running to see who is the busiest, most stressed, most needed. There's pressure to show your commitment to your job by putting in horrendous hours, even if they're not productive. That makes it hard for you to stick with your plan to get to the gym after work or to be home in time to cook a proper dinner. Who wants to be the one leaving the office at six when everyone else is trying for the "I stayed in the office till 3 a.m." award?

Financial commitments can also make things tricky. It would be great if you only needed to work a few hours to pay the mortgage, but that's not realistic, is it?

The benefits of balance

Clearly there are challenges in trying to have both a successful career and a great home and social life, but there are also enormous benefits in making it work. For starters, there's your health. If you're working unrelenting hours, not getting enough sleep, not eating well, and not getting any exercise, it's going to have a detrimental effect on your health. You can only run on adrenaline and caffeine for so long. By finding the time to fit sleep, food, and exercise into your life you'll not only stay healthier, but you'll be more productive (and happier) in the hours that you are at work.

Your relationships and emotional health also benefit from a better work–life balance. Research consistently shows that spending time with friends and family is an essential ingredient for happiness. Hanging out with friends and spending quality time with a partner are both great ways to relax. They take your mind off work and remind you that while work is important, it's not the only important thing in your life.

Finally, by freeing up some time from work commitments you're able to do the things that you've always said you'll do someday. These are likely to include the boring must-do things like cleaning out the spare room, the attic, or the mess under your bed, but you'll also have time for the cool things like the photography course you've been thinking about for ages or joining the local softball team like you've always said you would. There is something enormously satisfying about knowing that you're getting stuff done, expanding your horizons, and making the best use of your time.

Priority shift

*"When you first start work, you've got all of this energy and determination to do really well and impress. Then you do that for a few years and you get exhausted, and you realize that it's not really that big a deal. It's seems as though there is a much smaller percentage of people who still have career ambition and drive at 30. You get to a certain level of seniority and say, 'I'm happy with that.'" **Alison, 31***

What is it about reaching 30 (or thereabouts) that makes you rethink your priorities and place more emphasis on getting your work–life balance right? It might be exhaustion (ten years of working hard and playing hard!), or it might be a subtle shift in your priorities.

If you're approaching 30 and thinking (even vaguely) about settling down, starting a family, or renovating a home, or if someone you love has been sick or had some other worries, suddenly climbing the career ladder might not feel so essential. You might decide it's time to stop working incredibly long hours and start leaving work on time so you can paint the bedroom or visit your parents. You might start thinking less about career advancement and more about how you're going to combine your work with caring for a family.

This change in priorities can be subtle, almost unconscious. It might be that nothing obvious has changed in your life, but you just don't feel the same passion or energy for your job that you once did. You might feel that your career ambition has leveled out and you're happy to show up at work each morning, work hard, take a break at lunch, and leave it all behind at the end of the day.

Making a break for balance

"At this age we feel that we should be working hard and being successful, but who wants to spend all their time in the office and get stressed all the time? It's just not worth it. It's hard when you see everyone around you working really hard, but you've got to take control. It's your life." **Julie, 32**

So what can you do if you're working long hours and you don't have time to do the things that you would really like to be doing? How can you fight the temptation to do that little bit more at work, to check your e-mail over the weekend, or to say "yes" to the overtime when you know you should be doing other things? How can you take control and make a break for balance?

Things to try:

✦ **Check your hours.** Examine your working week and figure out what you spend your time doing. Write it all down. How much is "real" work? How much is lunch/ coffee/chat? How much is simply hanging around waiting for meetings to end or your boss to see you? Look for areas where you can save time. Look at what has become a habit rather than a need. For instance, if you have a late meeting once or twice a week, are you staying late on other days when you really don't need to?

✦ **Stop when it's "good enough."** Use the 80–20 rule. Instead of working to 100 percent perfection, stop when it is "good enough," or about 80 percent perfect. Assess whether that 20 percent is really going to make a big difference or whether you could have a bigger impact putting in that time and effort elsewhere.

✦ **Set expectations.** Start letting people know, firmly but politely, that you're not going to work all hours. Tell your boss you've finished your work and you're going home. If you've done the work you need to, you don't need to worry about disapproving looks!

✦ **Plan your time.** Sit down and make a list of all the things you want to do with your time. Include must-do things if you're going to get real satisfaction from getting them done, but also include plenty of doing-it-for-no-reason fun stuff. Make time for these things, ideally doing one a day. Try planning your week on a Sunday night or Monday morning, remembering to put in the stuff you really want to do first and then fitting the rest around it.

Working yourself into the grave

There are real health risks involved in working like a maniac and never giving yourself time out. Research from Canada suggests that 50 to 70 percent of doctors' visits are due to stress-related problems. In the United States they believe it's up to 80 percent!

Lots of people say that they work best under pressure, that they enjoy stress, and that's fair enough. Everyone has different tolerances. The stress of a deadline or the high expectations of a boss (or yourself!) can be challenging and motivating. But prolonged stress is never a good thing. If you're constantly in a highly stressed state (adrenaline pumping, heart rate high, brain going a mile a minute), you're running your body on overdrive. Keep this up and you'll face what's called "burnout"—a slowly evolving condition that causes you to just run out of physical and emotional energy.

Burnout—what to watch for:

✦ Feeling frustrated, angry, depressed, dissatisfied, and anxious at work on a regular basis.

✦ Getting moody or irritable over trivial things—things that didn't worry you in the past.

✦ Losing enthusiasm and motivation. You might find yourself thinking, "Why bother?" or "There's no point anyway."

✦ Relationship problems—both at home and at work. If you're feeling emotionally drained, it's hard to interact with others. If you do face conflict, you may be more likely to overreact with emotional outbursts. You're more highly strung and less tolerant of other people.

✦ Withdrawing from social contact. "Friends? What friends?"

✦ Health problems. If you're in a chronic state of stress, your physical resilience declines. You're much more likely to suffer from minor ailments such as colds, headaches, insomnia, and backache. You're also likely to feel generally tired and run-down.

✦ Substance abuse. Are you doing too much, too often?

Career Crisis 4: I'm looking for more.

Career crises at 30 are not just about feeling lost and confused, exhausted, or fed up with your job. One of the big challenges that you can face is being ready to take on more responsibility but not having the opportunity to do so. Are you ready to do more at work? Are you frustrated not because you haven't found the right career but because you're not using your full potential? Are you underworked, underpaid, or underappreciated? Or have you just found that you've scaled the learning curve and run out of challenges?

Being stuck in a job with no real prospects, being undervalued at work (financially or otherwise), or working for a boss who still sees you as too young and inexperienced for more responsibility can drive you mad. So mad, in fact, that you channel your frustration into looking for work elsewhere. "There must be someone else out there who will appreciate me," you mutter to yourself as you browse the recruitment Web sites.

But while finding a new job and telling your boss where to put the old one (metaphorically at least) can be very satisfying, if it's a knee-jerk reaction you can find yourself no better off than you were in the first place.

Another alternative is to stay in your current job and look around for other ways of reaching your goals. If you're looking to develop your skills or knowledge, you might consider further study. It's common for late 20- and early 30-somethings to rethink education, particularly those people who left school young or dropped out of college. Plenty of universities and other institutions offer courses that you can take part-time in the evenings, online, or via corres-pondence. If you're worried that you won't have opportunities because you lack the education, why not investigate your options and apply?

If you're frustrated because you can't seem to get ahead at work, it's also worth thinking laterally about your situation, like Susan . . .

Susan's story

*Soon after graduation, Susan started work at an invest-
ment bank and was doing well. Promotion time came
along and she expected to be promoted, no problem.
Unfortunately she wasn't, which upset her, and she
contested the decision, but no change was made. She was
told she would have to wait for another year. At first
Susan saw herself as a failure, not having moved upward
as quickly as she had hoped, but a conversation with a
coach helped her put her situation into perspective.*

*Susan's dream was to own her own business within five
years. As her coach pointed out, if that was her goal, what
difference did this promotion make? Very little, she realized. Susan decided to treat her missed promotion as an
opportunity to improve her skills. She managed to get
training in some of the areas her boss had identified as
needing development, and she found a number of
informal mentors around the business to help her. She got
promoted the next time around and then took a job at
another bank, one that was ultimately much better suited
to her interests and her long-term ambitions.*

Susan worked out what she really wanted and found help
within the company to move forward. The following tips
will help you if you want to do the same:

✦ **Decide what you want and why.** Think about what
   getting promoted means to you. Are you looking for
   recognition, status, or more money, or are you looking for

better opportunities and increased responsibility? Are there other ways of achieving these things?

✦ **Gather feedback.** Target your efforts by gaining specific feedback about what you need to do to get promoted or get into the job you want. Sit down with your manager and get a clear idea of what skills or knowledge you need to develop and the expectations you'll need to meet if you're going to work your way up the ladder. Next, develop a plan to address those areas. Keep your boss informed of your progress and achievements.

✦ **Find a mentor.** Mentors can be helpful if you find that you're not learning what you would like from your boss or others at work. A mentor can be anyone in your field (or even outside it) who has the skills and experience that you hope to develop yourself. A good mentor is someone you trust and respect and someone who's willing to share their time and expertise with you. Many people find that a past boss makes a good mentor. Is there anyone you have worked for from whom you think you could learn?

✦ **Uncover the rules of the game.** Promotion rarely works in the way it's supposed to. It's nice to think that good work will get you to the top, but often it helps to know the right people. Investigate how promotion actually works in your company. Talk to people who've progressed well and get their advice.

✦ **Build your profile.** Get to know other people at work. Join project teams or other groups to which you know you can make a contribution. By doing this you will build a network of people who will be impressed by what you can do and support you in your career. Also, consider joining a professional organization, and keep others informed of industry developments or any other information that they may find useful. They'll remember that you sent it, and you never know where it may lead.

Finally, if you're frustrated at work because you can't get ahead, because you're bored, or because you don't feel appreciated, remember that it's up to you to do something about it. Gone are the days in which you followed a predetermined career path and worked your way up the ladder with a pay rise at every step. These days you need to be more proactive about your career. You need to think about what you want from your work and to figure out how you're going to find it. The responsibility for your career rests squarely on your own shoulders. It's up to you to shape your career so that it works for you.

Making it happen at work

Now that you've explored your career dilemmas, it's time to work out your career goals. Look back to your profile from chapter 2 and your insights from the exercises in this chapter. What do you want to achieve career-wise? Write your goals below (remember to make them SMARTER). Once you're happy with them, begin your action plan. Soon you'll be moving toward a job you love. Remember that baby steps are best!

Exercise: Taking action at work

Career goals:

_____

_____

_____

_____

_____

_____

_____

_____

_____

_____

_____

_____

My career action plan:

1. _____

2. _____

3. _____

4. _____

5. _____

6. _____

7. _____

8. _____

9. _____

10. _____

Tips for career success

....

✦ **Make it real.** Achieving your goals is so much easier when you make them real. Think of your goal as a project and give it a name. Next, place project reminders around the house and your workspace. Stick a Post-it on your bathroom mirror or create a screensaver that reminds you of what you're planning to achieve. Bring your project to life in any way you can. If your goal is to leave the office at a respectable hour each night, set an alarm at your desk that will ring fifteen minutes before you plan to leave, and start packing up then and there.

✦ **Get over your fears.** Okay, you really want to go back to college to train as an architect, but the idea of giving up your income and committing several years of your life to studying is just too much. Your heart is saying, "I must become an architect if I'm truly going to enjoy my work," while your head is saying, "Don't kid yourself. How will you pay the rent, let alone save for vacation, if you pull that kind of stunt?" Think about what it is you're scared of. Is it the hard work that it will take to achieve your goal? Have you set yourself a goal that's too big? What can you do to break it down into smaller pieces that you can attack bit by bit? Take small steps toward your goal, and reward yourself for even the tiniest bit of progress. Find out whether you can take single architecture subjects in the evenings. Then see how you feel. Remember, your aim is to make a change in your life slowly but surely. If you're overly ambitious about what you can achieve, your fears could take over and you could end up going nowhere! But baby steps can lead to your perfect career.

CHAPTER 4
Love Life

Now and then . . .

At 30	At 20
✦ You worry about being alone.	✦ You were never alone.
✦ Your friends are getting married.	✦ Your friends were dating (each other).
✦ You're ready for commitment.	✦ Commitment?
✦ You obsess over your ex.	✦ You had no ex.
✦ You wonder whether this is "the One."	✦ You hoped this wasn't "the One."

Have you noticed how serious love has become? How weighty? Where's the Monday morning gossip about who hooked up with who at the club on Saturday night? What happened to the daily drama of your friends' love lives? When did you start discussing engagement rings, wedding plans, and bathroom design instead of bars and babes?

Love at 30. Whether you're settling down, splitting up, or steadfastly single, it's more intense than it was when you were 20. At 30 you've progressed from make-out-first-make-conversation-later. At 30 you're wondering whether you'll meet the guy or girl of your dreams and live happily ever after. At 30 you're agonizing over commitment and whether joint finances, family, and future will really bring lifelong contentment or whether you should bail out now while you've got the chance. At 30 it's not quite as carefree as it once was. This is the rest of your life we're talking about. It's time to get serious.

> *"Relationships are really hard at this stage. Some people are married and apparently happy, but I have two friends who have already divorced and they're only 30. The rest of us are either single or living with someone, and a lot of people are confused. They don't want to be alone, but they don't want to be tied down, either. Basically, they don't know what they want out of a relationship." **James, 31***

James is right. Relationships can be hard. The pressure is on to find someone and settle down, to knuckle down and make things work. Time's marching on, and your parents want grandkids (as they keep reminding you). You're sick of bars, clubs, and the single scene. But how do you find someone when all you do is work? And if you're with someone, how do you know if they are "the One"? Is there someone out there who's a better match for you? And if so, how do you break up after all this time, and can you face starting again?

In this chapter we'll look at how you can deal with your love laments at 30, whether you're single, confused, or grappling with commitment. Then, at the end of the chapter, you'll set goals for a happy 30-something love life.

Love Lament 1: When will I find someone to love?

Hands up if you thought your life would be "sorted" by the time you got to 30. You know, career established—check. Home owned—check. Loving husband or wife—check. Kids—check.

What happened?

Thirty may have come around a little fast, or maybe you're not the type to think that far ahead. Either way, the reality is that many of us don't have our love life sorted by 30. We're still single, thinking about the future, and looking for love.

"Most of my girlfriends, including me, thought, 'I'll be married with kids by the time I'm 30.' Then I kept lowering

the bar so that I could achieve it. As it got closer, I thought, 'Well, I'm not going to achieve that,' so I said, 'Okay, by 30 I'll be married,' then I thought, 'Okay, I'll be engaged.' Then it was like, 'Okay, by 30 I'll have a nice boyfriend I'll eventually get engaged to.' Now I've got six months left to go, with no prospects whatsoever!" **Claire, 29**

Oh, the pressure!

Single at 30 is perfectly acceptable (if not the norm), especially today, when there aren't the social rules that dogged our parents. In their day sex before marriage was basically unacceptable, and no one went to parties and other social events on their own. These days we've got the freedom to go out alone, and no one bats an eyelid if you're 28 and not married. In fact, by 30, when you're likely to have a bit more money and feel more comfortable in your own skin, single life in many ways is freedom, fun, and no responsibility.

So what's the downside?

The downside is complex. It has a little bit to do with time and a lot to do with expectations. If you see a family in your future, singledom at 30, no matter how much you love it, has an uneasy edge. If you're female, you're conscious that there's a use-by date on your procreating days. Medical science may have come a long way, but basic biology still dictates that if you want kids, you can't leave it until you're 50. It's not just a worry for the girls, either. Guys might not have the same biological deadline, but deep down they know that time is ticking by and that if they postpone kids for too long, they'll be too old and out of shape to throw a football in the backyard with them.

The sense that time is passing can be unsettling, and family and friends can add to the pressure. Your mom and dad may be dropping less than subtle hints about grandkids despite the fact there is not even the sniff of a boyfriend on the scene. Then there's peer pressure. Even the people you thought you could rely on to be single for years start to couple up and seem to be obsessed with finding out when you're going to do the same.

Someone to grow old with

"I'm tired of all this playing around. I want other things. Life is for sharing and I want someone to share mine with."
Simon, 29

The prospect of a family and the pressure from family and friends aren't the only things driving you to think more carefully about your single status at 30. You may not be considering children for a while, or at all, but most of us want to share our life with someone at some point. As 30 approaches, though, you might feel as though you're running out of places to look for them. There's a fear that all of the "good ones" are slowly disappearing. In your early 20s you seemed to meet someone new every day, and so many more of them were single. Now the girl from work you always meant to ask out suddenly gets engaged, or the sexy guy you had a fling with when traveling and always meant to call has fallen madly in love. With someone else.

So where are you now, love-wise? Are you searching for your life partner or just looking for someone to spend time with? What are you looking for in a love match? Would you know your perfect partner if you met him or her tomorrow? Do you really want someone at all? Are you happy on your own?

The answers to these questions make a big difference to how you go about finding someone.

Mark's story

Mark wasn't having much luck in the love department. He didn't have trouble meeting girls, mostly in bars after work. He'd gone out with two or three in the past year, but it had never worked out and he couldn't understand why. We asked Mark to visualize his life in five years' time with his perfect partner. He could describe the way she looked, sure, but more importantly we wanted him to describe what they were doing together—what a typical day looked like, where they were living, how they interacted, and who else featured in their daily life. Mark realized that while he was hitting the target when it came to meeting women, it wasn't the right target. He was sick of the singles scene, and what he really wanted was someone to plan a future with. The girls he met tended to be a few years younger, up for a good time, and certainly not interested in weekends in the country! He realized he needed to change strategy!

It's helpful to think about what you're really looking for in a relationship. A note of caution, though: do avoid creating a "perfect partner" checklist. You know the type of thing: good sense of humor, gorgeous, charming, kind, intelligent, witty, caring, loves cats, owns a mansion, great cook, good at buying diamonds, and so forth. The point is to understand the qualities that are most important to you in a partner, not to reel off an exhaustive list of attributes that must all be present. Relationships are made, not found, so if the basics are there, you're probably on to a good thing. She might not love bungee jumping quite as much as you, and she might even prefer to drink martinis rather than beer. He might wear deck shoes rather than trainers, or own a bicycle rather than a yacht. But are those reasons to dismiss someone you could build a relationship with?

Knowing what you want

So what do you really want? Find out with the following exercise. This is your chance to explore and clarify things that you might not have admitted to yourself or really known about yourself. It might take awhile, but knowing what you want can be very powerful and positive.

Exercise: Your ideal partner

Imagine your life with your ideal partner. Have a look back at your Perfect Future letter.

+ What can you learn from past relationships?

+ What values are you looking for in a partner? Look at your values in chapter 2.

+ What type of looks are you attracted to?

+ What would your day-to-day life be like?

+ How would you spend time with other people?

+ What sort of hopes and aspirations would you have as a couple?

Write it all down. Maybe leave it for a day or two and then come back to it. Write down any insights about what you really want.

My insights

_____

_____

_____

_____

_____

_____

_____

_____

What's in the way?

Even if you know what you're looking for, your lifestyle can get in the way of meeting new people. If you spend most of your waking hours staring at a computer, you hang around with friends you've known since you were four, and your favorite activity involves watching the latest incarnation of *Survivor* on TV every night, you're not likely to meet anyone new! There are of course so many upsides to being single that it can be much easier to carry on as you have been, even if you have a nagging feeling that you would actually like to be in a relationship. You might think that a relationship will come along when the time is right. It may well do that, but it's much more likely to happen if you give it a chance.

Try this:

Exercise: Practical obstacles to love

Are there any practical obstacles that prevent you from meeting people as often as you might? List your top five obstacles below. Don't worry about sounding silly or stating the obvious.

1. _____

2. _____

3. _____

4. _____

5. _____

What can you do to move these obstacles out of the way?

How can you make time and space for your love life? Instead of asking, "Why am I still single?" ask, "How can I meet someone?" Now might be the time to give up your solitary TV habit and make an appearance at your local bar or club. Can you finally say "yes" to the blind date your friend is always nagging you about? Or buy a new outfit to feel more confident? Or ban work on the weekends?

My thoughts

Think about how you're thinking

Practical things can get in the way of having the love life you'd like, but you may also be guilty of psyching yourself out of finding love. We all have negative beliefs about relationships, loosely based on bad experiences, seeing parents go through difficulties or divorce, our opinions of friends' relationships, or even things we've read. Thoughts like *"It's impossible to trust men"* or *"I'm not attractive enough to meet someone"* may be hidden away in the backs of our minds, and we may not always be aware of them, but they have a powerful influence over how we feel and what we do. For instance, if you believe *"I'll never find anyone like my ex,"* you're soon likely to compare any potential partners to your ex and look for things that support your belief. Not surprisingly, the new person won't be good enough in your eyes. Contrast this with a more helpful belief such as *"I'm open to new experiences."* This suggests you'll give things a try, and a good relationship may well come out of it.

Uncovering and rationally challenging negative beliefs can be helpful, as they often have no real substance to back them up. Once you realize that, you can start working on more helpful thinking.

Take Louise's example. She had been single for years—she'd had the odd fling or one-nighter, but nothing serious. She couldn't understand why nothing seemed to happen relationship-wise, and it was becoming increasingly frustrating. When Louise sat down and thought about what she was saying to herself about relationships she was surprised at the stuff she was coming up with. Things like, *"My last relationship didn't work out, so why should any other?" "If I am in a relationship, I will lose my independence," "You never meet anyone if you're looking,"* and *"Sex must be great every time."* We asked Louise to list the objective evidence for these beliefs and challenge them. Here's what she came up with for one of them:

Negative belief: My last relationship didn't work out, so why should any other?

Evidence for:

He left me after six months. (Challenge: There might have been other things going on. He wasn't happy with life generally.)

I did everything I could to make that relationship work. (Challenge: It proves I can put in effort. The fact it didn't work out wasn't just because of me; it needed both of us.)

Evidence against:

I have been in relationships that work, just not recently.

A couple of friends have had bad relationship experiences and gone on to meet people they're really happy with.

In fact, most people go through relationships that don't work out. It's just part of life.

More helpful belief: My last relationship is in the past and doesn't change that fact that I have a lot to give to a relationship.

By challenging her beliefs Louise found herself feeling much more open and receptive to meeting people. Whereas before she would dismiss people immediately on the basis of the most minute detail, like the color of their socks, now she noticed herself looking beyond the surface and trying to get to know people better.

Like Louise, you might have some blocking beliefs hidden away somewhere. Do your own exploration, get them out in the open and look at ways you can challenge and change them. It can take time for these beliefs to surface—don't forget that they may have been hidden away for years—but changing them is really worth the effort. It's time to argue with yourself.

Exercise: Relationship beliefs

What are you telling yourself about relationships? Make a list of anything that comes to mind.

_____

_____

_____

_____

_____

_____

_____

_____

_____

Take a look at your list. These are the beliefs that you're currently holding about relationships. Some of these will be more helpful than others. Circle the negative beliefs and pick the one you think gets in your way most of all. Apply some objective thinking to that belief by following these steps:

1. First think of all the hard evidence you have in support of that belief—only facts count here, not feelings!

2. Next write down all the objective evidence you have that contradicts the belief.

3. Then go back to the "evidence for." Challenge each piece of evidence. Is it really accurate? Is it really strong enough to base a belief on? Are there any alternative ways of looking at the situation?

4. Ask yourself how much you buy into the original belief. Chances are that your rational thinking will now let you accommodate a more balanced and helpful belief. Write down your new belief. Then note any actions you can take to support your new belief.

5. Have a look at these notes whenever you catch your negative belief creeping back into your mind. Remind yourself of how restrictive the belief is, and you'll find new energy to change it.

Negative belief:

_____

_____

Evidence for: | Evidence against:

_____

_____

_____

_____

_____

_____

_____

_____

More helpful belief:

_____

_____

_____

Actions to support new belief:

_____

_____

_____

Relax, what's the rush?

Finally, don't forget that you're still very young! It's so easy to be knocked off balance by the deluge of engagement announcements and wedding invitations that suddenly appear around the age of 30. It's tempting to think that everyone else in the entire world is permanently attached other than you and that you're running out of time. This pressure can mean that people rush into relationships and marriage before the time is really right for them. People who get together later in life have a much clearer idea of what they want based on their relationship experiences. In fact, the older people are when they marry for the first time, the less likely their marriage is to end up on the trash heap. So celebrate your single life and don't put too much pressure on yourself. There's plenty of time, and, ironically, the better you feel about being single, the more likely you are to meet someone. There's nothing more attractive than "I love my life" vibes.

Love Lament 2: We get along well, but is he or she really "the One"?

It's the million-dollar question. You've been with your partner for a while. You get along well but is he or she really "the One"—that special person you'll live happily ever after with?

This is one of the biggest love life challenges to hit

around 30. When you were younger you might not have thought about whether you wanted to spend the rest of your life with your boyfriend or girlfriend. Now, with your future life looming larger, you're more likely to be taking a closer look at your partner and trying to figure out if they're right for life.

"I'm living with my girlfriend; we've known each other for years and she's great to be with. There's nothing wrong with our relationship exactly, and we've ambled along together quite happily until now, but I'm starting to question whether it's right. My friends are starting to get married, and people are asking us whether we've got any plans. I don't think I can avoid this whole thing much longer. I mean, is she right for the long term or not? Do I want forever? I see some people who seem so head over heels—like a couple from work who are mad about each other and have moved in together after about three months. It's crazy. I just don't feel like that. No fireworks, no conviction. Is this how it really is, or am I settling for less than I should?" Richard, 28

Does she make me happy? Will he make a good dad? Is this really what I want? What is a good relationship really like? At 30 you often start to calculate whether a current relationship is the right place to invest your energy and conduct a mental review of your exes. Is current boyfriend Tim really better suited to you than Dan from marketing, or do you just feel more like settling down now than you did at 22?

Like Richard, how do you know whether your current

relationship is right if you feel you don't have enough to compare it to? How do you know when you've got enough experience to make any sort of decision? Do you feel the need to have kissed 1,000 toads before you meet your prince? Or are you in a panic because of the 30 deadline and think that it's too late to give up hope on a relationship you've invested so much time and effort in?

Searching for a "soul mate"

According to U.S. research, the vast majority of 20- to 29-year-olds list "soul mate" as the vital ingredient in a partner, implying complete emotional and spiritual compatibility. It seems that we are now after perfection.

Did your parents want the same thing, or was life simpler back then? People often seemed to be more interested in religion and economics and potential parenting ability. Now emotional connection is higher up the ranks than financial security or raising children. Expectations are rising, and you may be feeling the pressure to meet them.

As you search for your perfect relationship, relationship envy can turn you green. You go out for drinks with another couple and can only think about how they seem to get along so much better than you. But the chances are that the other couple, however "together" they look, are thinking the same about you. We tend to forget that every relationship is different; each has its strengths, weaknesses, and little quirks. Rather than looking outward at other relationships, no matter how tempting it is, it's important to focus inward on your own.

If you are in a state of relationship confusion, try this exercise:

Exercise: Relationship analysis

Step 1: Have a look at the following questions and write down any thoughts and insights below.

What do you love about your relationship? How can you have more of this?

What are your main concerns? What could you do to work these out?

What do you want for your partner?

What do you want from your partner? Are these expectations realistic? Can you get some of these needs met from other people?

Which relationships do you admire? What do you admire about them?

Take a look at your values. What are your partner's values? Which of your values are the same? Which are different? Can your value differences be resolved?

Look back at your Perfect Future letter. What do you want to achieve, in your relationship and in other areas of your life? Does this tie in with your partner's dreams? How can you move toward your dreams together?

How can you resolve any major differences in your personal styles?

My relationship insights

_____

_____

_____

_____

_____

_____

_____

_____

_____

_____

_____

_____

_____

Step 2: Talk to your partner. Communication is so important to a successful relationship. It's the easiest thing in the world to think you're the only one involved and often the hardest thing in the world to express how you feel. Share your thoughts and feelings and listen to those of your partner. Between you, you can reach a better understanding of what you both want and where your relationship is going.

It's easy to make your relationship the number one topic of conversation with your friends but the last thing you would dream of talking to your partner about. You can chat for hours with your friends, accompanied by several bottles of wine, and come up with insights or ideas that are forgotten as soon as you get home. Or you might just sweep any niggling concerns under the carpet by letting the day-to-day stuff keep you occupied. But the only way forward is to fight your fears and talk to your partner about how you feel. You might be feeling broody and think that your partner is much more interested in racing up the corporate ladder. Find out what he really thinks and what his dreams for the future are. Stop mind-reading. Once the two of you know what each other wants, both now and in the future, you can work out a way of getting there together. Your relationship is unlikely to transform overnight, but with time and effort the chances are that you can strengthen it and move forward.

Studies of married couples show that successful relationships have five times as many positive as negative moments together. The successful couples manage to keep their negative thoughts about each other—which are normal in any relationship—from overwhelming the positive ones. What's your ratio? How can you increase your positive moments?

It can be helpful to let go of the romantic ideal that there is only one person for all of us and to appreciate your relationship for what it is. If we believe in "the One," we're at risk of thinking that once we've found our golden ticket to happiness, the rest is plain sailing. It makes it easy to gloss over the reality that relationships require work and gives us an escape route. Sometimes it's easier to say, "It doesn't feel right anymore" and move on from a relationship than to learn more about what's not working and try to do something about it. However, if you find that you really don't know if things are going to work out between you, take a look at our next love lament.

Love Lament 3: My relationship isn't working out.

Given the changes that you go through in your late 20s and early 30s, it's no wonder that a lot of relationships hit the rocks. If you have been in a relationship that began in your early 20s, you have had to weather all sorts of changes. You start off with so much in common—the same experiences, friends, and interests. As your 20s progress, you may make new friends, your careers could diverge, and you might start to have different expectations of your relationship. If one of you suddenly decides they want to travel the world while the other is deep into establishing a career, it can be a challenge. More importantly, people become more aware of who they are in this period of their life, and differences become more apparent than they may have been before. Some relationships take this in their stride and last the course, but others break up. And whatever the reason, breaking up can be a painful time.

"I'd been with my girlfriend for years, but I'd always had some nagging concerns about our relationship that I'd put to the back of my mind. As the years went on they got worse, and in the end I couldn't ignore them. A friend from work gave me some very useful advice from his own experience. He told me to write down everything that was on my mind, break it down into the main issues, and talk to her about it. Which I did. It was one of the hardest things I've ever done, but it really helped. It actually confirmed my suspicions that we wanted very different things, and we're no longer together. I miss her, but I know that we had to go our separate ways, and I'm glad I took control of the situation."
John, 26

Thinking about breaking up can be scary. You don't want to hurt someone you love, and you're worried about doing the wrong thing. Most of all, you're concerned about whether you'll cope on your own. What will it be like? Will you ever meet anyone else? Is it better to stay in a relationship that you have invested time and effort in, even if you know it's not right, rather than be single? Will you feel like the odd one out because all your friends are in relationships? These feelings are likely to be stronger if you have been in the relationship for years.

If this is you, think carefully. If you want to be with someone, work at making it happen. Have you answered the "relationship analysis" questions in this chapter? Do you really understand the issues in your relationship? Can you resolve them? Have you tried? Have you got stuck in a negative view of your relationship? Can you remember and build on the positives?

If you really feel there is no way forward, then breaking up may be your only option.

Taking control

"I think from here I can do whatever I want. I'm very in control of my life. I don't know if becoming single at 30 kind of adds to that or if becoming 30 contributed to my wanting to be single!" **Lynn, 30**

Finding yourself single after a long relationship can be daunting, but it can also be incredibly exciting and positive. You'll find strength that you never knew you had and kindness from those around you. Give yourself time and space, and don't be afraid to cry on people's shoulders—you would do the same for them. Treat yourself well, and take some time to reflect on your bravery on making such a difficult life decision. With time you will find a positive side to a breakup even if you are on the receiving end.

If you want to make the most of your newfound single status, try following these tips for freedom and independence:

✦ **Write down all the things you'll be able to do that you couldn't do in your relationship.** Go traveling, study for a master's degree, spend all your money on yourself, run a marathon, go on vacations with your friends, move somewhere you've always wanted to but your partner didn't, reinvent your look, have what you want for dinner!

✦ **Think about all the people that you will be able to spend more time with.** These might be the same people that you go to for help and support when you're feeling lonely or down. Call them up and reestablish friendships that may have fallen by the wayside while you were in your relationship.

✦ **Remember all the reasons why you want to break up.** When it actually comes to making the break, these often seem to disappear from your mind, and it fills up with romantic images and happy memories.

✦ **Respect the time you spent together.** You might find yourself unable to resist the temptation to bad-mouth your ex to anyone who will listen. Bear in mind that by doing this you can undermine the time you spent in the relationship. Think of your relationship like a house, or a vacation. It may not have lasted forever, but you enjoyed it while you were there.

✦ **If all else fails, take a trip to the Lovesick Pub in Bangkok** . . . where jilted lovers can throw empty bottles at pictures of their exes! Other facilities include a crying room and a screaming room. The louder you scream, the brighter the lights get! To top things off there's a shop where you can sell all the gifts your ex gave you and pocket the cash. It might be worth the airfare for such a cathartic experience!

Love Lament 4: The "M" words give me cold feet!

Moving in, marriage, and mortgages. Do these ideas inspire passion or fear? Or both? A common dilemma as we turn 30 is the double-edged view of commitment. We can find ourselves caught somewhere between the past and future. On the one hand we want the freedom of the past, and on the other we want the security that the future seems to offer. And it seems that there is typically a bit of a male/female divide driven by women's biology. The girls are one step closer to the security end of the scale, whereas their boyfriends are likely to be suffering from cold feet and want to cling to their independence for a while longer.

However, there is a definite upside to marriage. Married people (even the young ones) are happier and healthier, live longer, and have lower rates of a variety of psychological problems. Men, take note: as a rule you benefit more from marriage than women do. Married women are only slightly better off than unmarried women, but unmarried women are considerably healthier and happier than unmarried men!

Domestic bliss

Here are some tips for surviving some of the "cold feet" challenges of committed grown-up relationships:

+ **"I'm not ready to say 'forever'."** To labor a stereotype, women can be very pro-marriage as 30 approaches. For some women, marriage means getting a diamond, dressing up like a princess, having a big party, and feeling secure in their relationship. They're likely to make this known to their other halves, who then feel under pressure to ask the big question. If you find yourself in a situation like this, have an open conversation with your partner about how you feel. Explore your feelings about long-term commitment, whether this means moving in, buying a house, or marriage. Come to a compromise that you're both comfortable with.

> *"To be perfectly honest, I didn't care about getting married too much. But I knew that she had had this dream of dressing up in a big meringue since she was about six, and I wanted her dream to come true."* **Mark, 31**

✦ **"I don't want to give up all of my freedom."** You don't have to. There's no need to give up all your friends and the stuff that you like to do just because you're living with someone or getting married. In fact, it's really important that you keep a life outside your relationship. How will you make sure that happens?

✦ **"The relationship will become boring if we see each other all the time."** Only if you let it. Relationships involve hard work, and unless you make an effort, the domestic drudgery will overtake the sparkle and passion. Go on dates together, even if it's just to the local bar. Make special time for your relationship every day. And remember all the pluses involved in seeing each other more—waking up together, having unexpected cuddles, and reading the papers together on a Sunday morning.

✦ **"What do we do about money?"** Research by UK relationship experts Relate shows that money issues are the main reason why people divorce and that 40 percent of couples rate money as their chief cause of disagreement. So it's worthwhile getting things straight from the start. Attitudes about money differ vastly, and talking about yours is a good starting point. You can then work out a way of organizing your money that you're both happy with.

Very Harlequin Romance

"We were away skiing and had been on the slopes all day. My boyfriend started acting very strangely and dragged me back up the mountain again. We got there just as it was getting dark, and he pulled out an engagement ring! He was disappointed, though, as the lady in the shop had told him that the diamond looked best in sunlight, and by the time he'd plucked up the courage to ask me, it was dark and you couldn't really see it!"

"We went to the beach for the weekend, to the little beach house that we'd bought a few years ago. I don't think she suspected a thing; it was just a normal weekend away as far as she was concerned. After a romantic walk along the beach, I popped the question! She was delighted! I was so worried about getting a ring that she wouldn't like, but she hasn't stopped talking about it to her friends, so I think I did okay!"

"It was Christmas Day, and at the bottom of a big box was

> *a card saying, 'Would you like to be Mrs. Ryder?' and a ring stuck to the card with tape. I thought it was a ring from a Christmas cracker and some sort of cruel joke, as he knew I wanted to get married but always said he wasn't going to ask for at least another five years. Turned out he was serious, and it was a real engagement ring!"*

Making it happen in love

Now that you know more about what you really want from your love life, you can set relationship goals and create an action plan. Do this in the same way that you did for your career. Your goals could be about being more comfortable with your single status, meeting new people, or moving forward in your current relationship. What is going to raise your Pizza of Life score for relationships and get you closer to that Perfect Future? What can you do tomorrow to be happier with love?

Exercise: Taking action in love

Love life goals:

_____

_____

_____

_____

_____

_____

_____

_____

_____

_____

_____

_____

My love life action plan:

1. _____
2. _____
3. _____
4. _____
5. _____
6. _____
7. _____
8. _____
9. _____
10. _____

Tips for luck in love

....

+ **Fight your inner critic.** Remember that keeping a positive attitude makes all the difference when working toward goals. We all have an "inner critic" inside us, a voice that criticizes us incessantly. Chances are that your inner critic is chattering away right now, saying, "There's no point asking her out, you'll only embarrass yourself" or "If I try and talk to him, we'll just end up having a fight" etc., etc. Sound familiar? But if you pay attention to the criticism and challenges, you expect the worst and start to behave in a way that fulfills those expectations— maybe you will decide not to ask people out, or will avoid having conversations with your partner about your relationship. That's no good for you. The good news is that you can defeat your inner critic—and here's how. Imagine your own best friend. You want the best for her and are totally on her side. You support her, encourage her and are always there for her. Your challenge is to be your own best friend. Stop listening to the inner critic. Argue with it! Treat yourself like a precious best friend. Believe you can make changes, and encourage yourself to do so. It will make all the difference to both your happiness and your success.

+ **Use what you've got.** Your strengths, personality, and values are key to making things happen. Draw on what you have learned so far. What strengths can you use to help you meet new people? Try using curiosity, for example, to ask questions and find out about people, or humor to break the ice. What aspects of your personality can help you move forward? If you are creative, you can use that to overcome problems and obstacles that stand in your way. Knowing yourself also helps you to believe in yourself. It provides the hard evidence that you need to fight your inner critic and reach your love life goals.

CHAPTER 5

Nearest
& Dearest

Who do you call when . . .

You need fashion advice for a hot date?

_____

You've had a particularly bad day at work?

_____

You're lost and need to know how to get somewhere?

_____

Your washing machine has broken down?

_____

You just need cheering up?

_____

Who are your nearest and dearest? The people you call to celebrate your successes or share your worries? Close relationships are an important part of what makes life worth living and contribute greatly to happiness. What's happening to yours?

As we turn 30, our relationships with family and friends often start to change. By then we are less emotionally and financially dependent on our parents (in some cases!), and instead of running home, throwing a tantrum, and blaming them whenever life doesn't go our way, we start to find ways of coping on our own and depending on our partners and friends instead. We are usually better able to deal with the expectations that our parents tend to place on us— or at least more used to living with them—and our relationship with our parents also changes because we see them getting older and may want to build a closer relationship with them.

At the same time, maintaining friendships can be a challenge. Around the age of 30, people start to have different priorities, and friendship patterns start changing. "Friendshift" kicks in. In our early 20s we usually have lifestyles that are similar to those of our friends, so friendships are easier to keep up. By 30, with the addition of babies, careers, travel, and partners, it can prove more difficult. To add to this, you may have to get to know your partner's friends—a whole new set of people to weave into your social network.

Here is your chance to take a good look at your close relationships and figure out how to make them even better than they are already. In this chapter we look at the main friends and family scenarios that might contribute to your Turning 30 Blues and what you can do to turn them around. Whether it's seeing people more or changing the way you spend time with them, you'll soon be on the road to making the most of the close relationships in your life.

Family Scenario 1: My relationship with my parents is changing.

As you turn 30 the fact that your parents may not be around forever may become more of a consideration in your life. Parents are getting older—and perhaps more eccentric! They may start to take it easier and prepare for retirement. And for those of you lucky enough to still have grandparents, they're probably coming to the end of their long lives. Unlike the grandparents you never met or who passed away when you were very young, those who are still around as you reach 30 have always been around, and it can be so very hard to imagine life without them. While they are still here, it's up to you to make the best of the time you have with them.

You might make some important decisions so that you can be closer to your parents as they get older. Emma, 28, came to us in a dilemma about whether to stay in the UK or whether to move back to her native Australia. The thing she kept coming back to was her parents:

"Living in a different country is hard because I can't be with my parents. And although I love living abroad, I don't think I'll do it forever, because I want to be there for my parents when they need me."

Emma clearly wanted to be near her parents, but her focus was on them needing her rather than the other way around. For many of us, this is when the fact that we are adults really hits home. It hits even more quickly and sharply if one of our parents becomes seriously ill or if we lose a parent. The reality of life as a precious and fragile entity becomes apparent, and we feel the need to make the most of each moment. Of course this can happen well before 30, but that age can be a time of serious reflection and reprioritization when people concentrate on the important people in their lives.

Appreciation

The following exercise is fantastic for showing your parents, or anyone else close to you, how much you care about them. They will bask in your appreciation, and you will have the chance to express your gratitude. Gratitude is a powerful emotion and helps us to focus on the good things in our lives. It is the backbone of strong relationships.

Exercise: Saying thank you

Write a letter to someone in your family or to a friend who is important to you. Write about concrete things—what that person has done for you and how it has affected you. Include fond memories and things that make you happy. Make some notes below, then write them up into a letter.

_____

_____

_____

_____

_____

_____

_____

_____

_____

_____

_____

_____

_____

_____

_____

_____

_____

_____

_____

_____

_____

_____

Once you have written your letter, ideally take it to the person, read it aloud, and leave it with them as a gift. If you feel uncomfortable doing that, just send it and follow up with a call.

Family roles

Are you stuck in a childhood role? Some people easily move into adult relationships with their parents, while others get stuck in patterns of behavior from their childhood. So, even if you have fulfilled your parents' expectations and have a flourishing career, your own house, and even your own family, you revert to being a five-year-old around your parents. Or maybe you play a certain role in your family and you're getting frustrated by it. If this sounds like you, try the following exercise:

Exercise: Growing up

Try answering the questions below—they will help you take action to shake off the terrible-teenager you. Write down any insights in the space provided.

What are your normal patterns of behavior with your parents? Are you the wonder-kid who got straight As and has to remain a high achiever? Or are you still playing the role of the black sheep who could never do anything right?

_____

_____

_____

_____

_____

_____

_____

_____

How can you break out of these patterns? How could you relate to your parents differently?

_____

_____

_____

_____

_____

_____

_____

_____

What do you have in common with your mom and dad? Look back at your values. Are these similar to those of your parents? What interests do you have in common? How can you use these similarities to change your relationship from parent–child to two adults relating on an even footing?

_____

_____

_____

_____

_____

_____

_____

_____

_____

Family Scenario 2: I can't deal with the pressure!

"When are you going to meet someone suitable, stop wasting money, start saving for a pension, etc., etc.?" Is there a voice in the back of your head that sounds very much like your parents? Or is your mom or dad actually saying these things to you?

Parents often want to see you earning a decent living and secure in a long-term relationship, preferably complete with marriage certificate and babies. They may be applying their "rules of life" to you and missing the point that the world is a very different place from the one they grew up in. The only difference they may see is the wealth of opportunities—which they see as wonderful rather than stress-inducing—and so they may say, "You're clever, why don't you go on one of those millionaire shows and make some money?" or "You're a good cook, why can't you be a celebrity chef?" They're convinced that things are much easier now than in "their day." In many ways they are, as in the past most people had to work hard for a living and didn't have the opportunity to become overnight millionaires or celebrity chefs. But all these opportunities can bring pressure, too—the stress of making the right choice among millions, the idea that if you don't have it all, you're some sort of failure. And your parents may be able to see only the positives in the social changes that have taken place since they were your age, not the challenges. So they expect you to do the same as they did, only quicker and better.

Not surprisingly, these expectations can have a massive impact on us. We often can't help wanting the approval of our parents, no matter how old we are, and feel that by now they should be impressed with us. If they aren't, it can be difficult to come to terms with.

Different choices

"I come from an Asian family, and my parents have very clear views of what they want me to do. That is, marry someone Asian they approve of and settle down and have babies. I'm so confused, because that's not what I want to do. I've grown up in a western world where people make their own choices and I want to do the same, but I can't bear the thought of upsetting my parents. It's really difficult when your expectations are so far from those of your parents." *Serena, 27*

Like Serena, there may be religious or cultural reasons behind what your parents want for you, and it can be very difficult to challenge the ideals and beliefs that define the way that they live.

There is no right or wrong way to deal with this; everyone is different. In chapter 1 you identified the expectations that others, including your parents, have of you. You also chose which of these you would like to live up to and which to discard. It may not always be possible to get your parents to see it your way. Some of you may decide to give up your way for theirs—Serena knows in her heart that she will probably do what her parents want and do her best to make it work. Many of you, however, will choose to go your own way and follow your own dreams. In that case, be prepared to deal with some resistance to your plans as your parents come to realize that their expectations may not be met.

> "At 25 I decided I wanted to travel for a bit. I knew Dad would disapprove, as he strongly believes that people should always be employed and financially responsible. I explained that many people traveled right after college, but I'd gone straight to work and now I wanted some time out. I told him that many companies saw this as a good thing and I wouldn't have a problem getting a job when I got home, but as expected, he didn't react too well. I was upset and considered changing my plans. But as I thought about it, I realized we just held very different beliefs. He'd grown up in a world where having a secure job was the most important thing. In my world it's okay to take time out, and getting a mortgage as soon as possible isn't the point of living. Even if he couldn't quite see it my way, he still loved me. So I went. And at the airport, he waved me good-bye with a tear in my eye." **Anita, 27**

Family Scenario 3: Do I want a family of my own?

Babies. As 30 approaches they become something that you could have rather than something you once were. In fact, as you turn 30 you may well hit the "baby stage." You're in a serious relationship, maybe married, and everyone from your mom to your dentist is asking the baby question.

People are having babies later and later—the average age of a first-time mother in the U.S. is now 25.1, compared with 21.4 in 1970. A recent study by London University's Institute of Education found that 63 percent of fathers of babies born today are over 30, as are 53 percent of mothers. You may already be a parent, but for those who aren't, 30 seems like a biological milestone when it comes to having kids. So what might be going through your mind as you approach this big decision?

"I got married last year, and the next obvious thing to do was to have kids. There was no question in my mind about it; it felt like the right thing to do, the logical next step. But now that the time has come to start trying, it feels quite different and I'm questioning whether I'm truly ready to give up my independence and free time. No more sitting around with the papers on Sunday mornings or having dinner with friends at a moment's notice. There's this feeling I get when I hold a baby, and there's no doubt in my mind that I want one. But do you ever feel ready to give your life up? It's a hard decision. I've started to make a list of all the things I want to do before having kids, and I intend to check them off!" Natalie, 29

Perfect parenthood?

Like Natalie, can you see two sides of the story? On the plus side, there's the miracle of creating another human being, someone to cherish and delight in. You'll be building your own family unit and taking a leap toward the real responsibility of adulthood. You imagine that having a baby will bring you closer to your partner and will be the start of a bright new future.

On the other side of the coin things look quite different. Horror stories from friends come to mind—no sleep, endless diaper changing, the complete absence of time for yourself and the pressure of real responsibility. Depending on one salary or finding the cost of child care can also be concerns. This image of parenthood doesn't quite cut it. But the reality is that you don't think you can put the decision off for much longer, given that the biological clock is ticking. So what do you do?

Exercise: Weigh it up

If you're seriously considering having children, consider the following questions and talk them over with your partner. Like any major life decision, take the time to understand the situation and create your "case for change." The idea of having children is embedded in our society and is the expected next step in a serious relationship after the house-buying/marriage step. Added to this is the pressure of the biological clock as 30 approaches. But the following questions can help you decide whether having a child is right for you at this point in your life:

What are your reasons for having children?

What are you excited about?

What are your concerns?

How do you feel about raising kids?

What financial and working arrangements would be necessary?

What are your thoughts on parenting?

My thoughts

_____

_____

_____

_____

_____

_____

_____

_____

_____

_____

_____

_____

_____

_____

_____

Friends Scenario 1: I never see my friends anymore.

Turning 30 can be a lonely time. You might find that your friends seem to have moved on and would rather spend cozy, couply nights in on a Saturday, whereas you're still up for a mammoth drinking session. One minute you're going out with your friends, and the next they've turned into unrecognizable people who go on weekends at the beach or attend political rallies or love flamenco dancing. Suddenly their new boyfriends or girlfriends are the center of their universe, and you're left floating around alone or feeling that three's a crowd.

"I've got a few really close friends who I've known since I was about 12. We've always been around for one another despite doing our own thing and living in different places. But now I'm finding myself a bit isolated from them, as they all seem to have moved on to the 'next stage' in life. They're married, have bought houses that they're working on all the time, and a couple of them even have babies. It makes it impossible to catch up, even on the phone, as they're trying to deal with work, kids, and partners. And when we do talk, their conversation revolves around a set of priorities that I can't get my head around. Sash windows, gardening, baby clothes—they're just not topics I'm familiar with! My friends will always be close to me, but maybe I need to try to meet more people who are on my wavelength, and who I can socialize with more regularly." Amy, 31

When we are younger, life can pretty much revolve around friends, but by 30 reality can feel quite different. People move away to work, to be with partners, to set up families, to see the world. The ideas you had about seeing all your friends in the same bar on a Saturday night are replaced by infrequent phone calls and the occasional catch-up at people's weddings.

Also, whereas before you probably had a core group of friends, now you're likely to socialize in smaller groups. The big clubbing nights may give way to dinner parties, Saturday lunches, or quick drinks after work. It's all too easy to sit back and complain that you never see anyone anymore and to blame them for being too baby/boyfriend/decorating obsessed.

If you're feeling the need for friendship as you turn 30, try out our ideas for making some small changes that can have a big impact.

Friendship first

Things to try:

✦ **Go for coffee.** A couple of hours on a Saturday afternoon can be much easier for people to make than Saturday night drinks. Or how about brunch on Sunday? Try new ways of getting together and find one that works.

✦ **Be prepared.** Planning and structure can help enormously. It's easy to get into the routine of working late, having dinner, watching TV, and going to bed. Weeks fly by without your seeing the important people in your life.

How about putting a regular slot in your week for seeing your friends and building the rest around that? That way it's a priority for you and everyone else, and other stuff can be planned around it. Or arrange a weekend away together, even if it's in six months' time, so that you have a special time together to look forward to.

✦ **Keeping in touch.** E-mails, phone calls, letters, text messaging—there are so many ways of keeping in touch now that even if your best friend is traveling the world, there's no reason why you can't share the journey with him or her.

✦ **Meet new people.** If you've moved somewhere new or feel that your friends have moved on, it could be time for some new people in your life. List all the places you could meet new people—through work, neighbors, the Internet, professional organizations, community projects, vacations, evening classes. Try that hat-making or Japanese or knitting class. Do something small every day next week toward your goal of finding new friends—volunteer to organize a work night out, chat with a colleague, look up evening courses on the Web. Each action will move you along and build your confidence.

Friends Scenario 2: How do I fit in with my partner's friends?

Are you in a new relationship as you approach 30? If so,

you may have recently been introduced to a whole new set of people through your partner. This might be great for some people, but others can get caught up in a dilemma. On the one hand you want to make an effort with people your partner cares about, on the other you resent spending time with people you wouldn't choose to otherwise.

People deal with this type of friends scenario in different ways. Some find it easy to fit in, yet others find the whole idea of getting to know new people, or "surface socializing," totally stressful. Either way, most of us end up making social sacrifices for the one we love. If this works both ways, great. If not, and one of you is having all the fun while the other looks on, you could have an argument or two on your hands.

"I feel less tolerant now and so can't be bothered to start again with people—you know, find out their shoe size, the names of their parents, what they do for a living, etc. But the alternative's not much better, because if you don't do that, you have to make small talk, which generally consists of boring topics such as the color they're going to paint their bathroom. It's really not my idea of fun. I guess because you haven't chosen them as your friends, they aren't necessarily your type of people, and because you kind of feel it's been forced upon you, you feel annoyed. I find myself doing so much fake laughing and smiling that my cheeks really hurt." **Helen, 27**

Apart from the social pressure, you may also start to have secret concerns about your partner—what does it say about them if they have annoying friends? Of course, this doesn't mean your relationship is doomed, even though it might seem like it. It's unlikely that you're going to like all the same people. This is true of your friends, too. How often have you looked at one of your close friends and not been able to understand why they get along so well with a certain person? But it doesn't mean you stop being close to them. The same can apply to you and your partner.

What's yours is mine

If you are having problems with your partner's friends, here are some tactics that could be the answer you're looking for:

✦ If you dislike your partner's friends, think about why. One of the reasons may be that they reflect qualities you don't want to see in your partner. You might see your boyfriend's buddies as unreliable, for example, or have no time for your girlfriend's frivolous friends, and secretly be afraid that your partner is just the same. Also, once you've taken a dislike to someone, it's all too easy to focus on the qualities you don't like rather than look for anything positive. To get past this, try to make the effort to understand why this person and your partner are friends.

✦ If your partner knows a whole group of people and you find this intimidating, find one person in the group who you like and get to know them better. That way, you can look forward to seeing them every time you go out.

✦ If mixing friends simply doesn't work for you, you can always see your friends separately. There are no rules to say you should socialize together all the time. If evenings with your boyfriend's friends talking about sports are starting to drive you insane, stop going! There may be some people you see as a couple and others you see separately. Find out what works best for you.

+ Get your friends and your partner's friends to make friends too. Organize a party, equipped with loads of food and drink, and people will start to get to know one another. They get a chance to meet new people, and you solve your problem!

Friends Scenario 3: Who are the important people?

Are you suffering from friends overload? By the time you reach 30 you've met so many people from different places—school friends, college friends, people from different jobs, traveling and friends of friends. As we go through life we seem to collect people along the way. In our 20s spending every evening out with a different group of people may seem a great way to live. As 30 approaches, other areas of our lives may take priority, such as more serious relationships and career commitments. We can find that we've reached our friendship capacity and that we just don't have enough time and energy for all the people in our lives. This is often a time when you start questioning whom you really want to spend time with. Who are the important people for you?

"My life is whizzing by at such a fast pace, and I'm finding myself unable to keep up! I'm a very extroverted and sociable person—I love being with people and have loads of fun with my friends, but lately I've found that the number of people in my life has just gone crazy and I'm left with no time to myself. There are my friends from home, and work, and the campaigning that I do, and yoga, and friends of friends. It's getting to the stage when I'm trying to fit two or three things in practically every night of the week. I just can't say no to people, and I do like them all." Jane, 31

Like Jane, you might find yourself with a bursting social calendar that's booked up weeks in advance. You like people and feel you should keep in touch with everyone you meet. But is it getting to be too much? What do you do if you find yourself buckling under the pressure of too many social ties?

If this is you, stop and turn off your cell phone. (Go on, you can do it!) It's time to take control of the relationships in your life with the "friendship test."

Exercise: Friendship test

Step 1: List all the people in your social network below.

_____

_____

_____

_____

Step 2: "Friendship test" each person on your list by asking yourself the following questions. These will help you decide how much effort you really want to be putting into each of these relationships.

When they call, are you genuinely pleased to hear from them?

Do you feel pleased and energized after seeing them?

Can you see yourself being friends with them in ten years' time?

Would they be on your list of five people to call when you need help or when something goes well for you?

What would your life be like if they weren't in it?

This test will help you to get some perspective on the people in your life. The question "Do you feel pleased and energized after seeing them?" is interesting, as you might find there are some people in your life who really don't make you feel like this. These might be people you've known since you were young and maintained a friendship with based on the past, or people you've come to know through other friends and somehow hung on to. Is it worth still hanging on to them?

Once you have worked out who are the most important people in your life, it's also worth thinking about how you spend time with them. Do you see your best friend only in big groups where it's difficult to have a proper conversation? Could you suggest having a weekly dinner as well so you have a regular chance to get together and chat?

Friends envy

Ever felt possessed by the green-eyed monster at the mere thought of a friend's career or relationship success? Ever watched a friend drive away in his new sports car and envied his salary? Ever wished you were able to work from home like your friend does? Envied the diamond on your best friend's finger?

If you're not getting satisfaction from your own life, it's tempting to covet the work, relationships, and success of your friends. In fact, even if you're happy with your own life, there's always someone nearby who seems to be doing just that little bit better.

When you're dealing with the Turning 30 Blues it's very easy to look at your friends' successes, hoping that they will be able to give you the answers to the conundrums you are facing. It certainly seems easier than peering into your own muddled heart and mind. But friends envy is a dangerous activity. First, we all tend to compare ourselves to those friends who are doing "better" than us in some way, and we quickly gloss over the areas in which they are struggling.

Secondly, we forget that what suits one person doesn't necessarily suit another. Your friend with the

> sports car might get paid well, but deep down, do you really think you're suited to his line of work?
>
> Finally, if you're faced with the green-eyed monster, remind yourself that that person is a friend you love, respect, and want the best for. Be pleased for him or her.

Making it happen with nearest & dearest

So what changes would you like to make in your relationships with the people who are important to you? Are you interested in strengthening existing friendships or creating new ones? Do you want to make an effort with your partner's friends or shake up your social life using insights from your friendship test? Maybe your family is your focus instead—building adult relationships with your parents or even preparing for a family of your own. Write your goals and actions below.

Exercise: Taking action with nearest & dearest

Nearest & dearest goals:

_____

_____

_____

_____
_____
_____
_____
_____
_____
_____
_____
_____
_____
_____
_____
_____
_____
_____
_____
_____

My nearest & dearest action plan:

1. _____
2. _____
3. _____
4. _____
5. _____
6. _____
7. _____
8. _____
9. _____
10. _____

Tips for nearest & dearest success

....

✦ **Trust your instincts.** Use your intuition. This isn't an easy thing to define, and it's like a muscle that you need to keep using to build up. Still, it's very useful. So, when you're making changes in your life, pay attention to your gut feelings. There's a good chance that they're telling you something important. They tend to be the compass that points you in the direction that is right for you, the one that reflects your values, strengths, and personal style. They may draw you toward some people and away from others. Learn to listen to them.

✦ **Accept ups and downs.** Motivation is never consistent, and you shouldn't expect it to be. One day you might be on top of the world and full of enthusiasm for your new social life, the next you might be wondering what possessed you to think that you could ever change anything at all. It's important on your down days not to give up altogether. If you're having a rough time, be kind to yourself, take a tiny baby step toward your goal that day, and wait for the wave of enthusiasm to pick you back up tomorrow.

CHAPTER 6

Leisure, Pleasure & Healthy Living

> ✦ Your psychological health is steadily improving now that you're 30.
>
> ✦ But your physical fitness is declining and your basal metabolic rate—the rate at which you burn calories at rest—has already started its downward slide.

Life can be complicated at 30. You work seventy hours a week, go to the gym, socialize at night, go away on weekends and study for extra qualifications whenever you can find spare time. If you own your own home, you're either renovating or decorating or both, and there's an endless stream of household chores requiring your attention. On top of this you're expected to see your parents, pay your bills, wash your clothes, save your money, and clean out your refrigerator (occasionally at least).

"I love my life, but there is so much going on. I'm at the gym at 6:30 a.m., I work until 7 p.m., go out with friends after work, and rarely get to bed before midnight. My parents want to see me on the weekend, and I want to catch up with friends. As well as working I'm studying part-time, so I have to fit that in somewhere, and of course there's cooking and cleaning to be done. I'm saving to buy a house, but it's hard to resist the temptation to spend my money, especially when there's so much cool stuff to buy. Then there's a car to run, cell phone bills, vacations . . . I don't know how I'll ever afford a family of my own, or when

*I'll find the time. I don't get enough time to think about MYSELF!" **Amanda, 30***

In this situation it's easy to feel guilty—guilty about doing too much, about not doing enough, guilty about what you do, and definitely about what you don't do. You feel guilty about what you eat, whether you're working as hard as you should be, whether you should be seeing the world, seeing your friends, or just plain whether you're getting as much out of life as you could.

And all this racing around may be taking its toll on more than just your mind—you may also thinking about your physical state, possibly for the first time. You may be fending off extra pounds, or worrying about the state of your skin, or your gray hair, or lack of hair, or both. If you're the sporting type, you might have noticed that your body no longer does what it used to. Or if it does, it makes sure that you know about it the next day. And hangovers may be increasingly hard to bear.

You're also caught in leisure limbo. Around the age of 30 can be an in-between time when you don't want to quite let go of clubbing, but you're not really ready for a life of theater trips, dinner parties, and beige cardigans. But it can also be a time of finding what suits you as an individual and deciding how, given a choice, you want to spend your time. That is, if you have any! Surrounded by the lure of the "be everything, have everything, do everything" lifestyle, when do you find the time to look after yourself, relax, and stay healthy? How do you get off the treadmill and take a moment every once in a while to smell the roses?

In this chapter we look at leisure, pleasure, and healthy living. We talk about how you can make the most of the leisure time you do have. We also consider how, while your free-time activities might be changing as you get older, they play an important part in keeping you sane. Speaking of sanity, we take a look at the importance of staying healthy, both physically and emotionally, and by the end of this chapter you will have set goals for a healthier, more interesting and balanced lifestyle.

Lifestyle Challenge 1: How can I get the best from my leisure time?

Now that you're turning 30, what are you doing with your free time? Do you hit the day spa or the sports field? Do you indulge in retail therapy or while away the hours with friends at the bar? Do you make it out of the house at all? Do you make it out of bed?

> *"I spend all week looking forward to the weekend so that I can just veg out, sleep in, and watch TV, but by Sunday afternoon I'm usually moody and irritable. What's going on there?"*
> **Sharon, 29**

Time out from your responsibilities is vital to your

happiness. Free time gives you the chance to do the things you want to do, rather than the things you have to do. It gives you the time to switch off and not worry so much about what's going on at work or elsewhere, and it helps you to rejuvenate, giving you the energy to get stuck back into everyday life with renewed focus.

But it's easy not to use your leisure time to best effect. You might think that any time out is good for you, but in fact leisure activities are not all equal in the happiness stakes. While vegging out in front of the TV, reading *People* magazine, and even sex all make you feel good momentarily, they don't necessarily give you the same sense of long-lasting happiness that you get from hobbies, exercise, or doing something that requires a bit of effort and a degree of mental activity.

In fact, research shows that the state induced by passively watching television is similar to a mild form of depression! That's because time off is often just empty time, and empty time gives you time to worry. So you turn on the TV for distraction, and a few hours later you go to bed not feeling any better than you did before.

Using your free time to do things that challenge you (a bit at least) is the best way to get a sense of relaxation and renewal. It distracts you from whatever is on your mind, gives you a sense of achievement and a feeling of control, and ultimately makes you feel happier, reenergized, and ready to start again.

Think for a moment. What were you doing the last time you had a really invigorating weekend and felt ready to get back to work on Monday morning?

Exercise: The day has come!

If you don't feel that you're making the most of your free time, try this exercise:

Step 1: Write down absolutely every weird and wonderful thing that you've ever seen, read, or heard about and said, "I'd love to do that someday." You know, "Someday I'll write a book, run a marathon, go skydiving…"

Things I will do someday:

_____

_____

_____

_____

_____

_____

_____

_____

_____

_____

_____

_____

_____

_____

_____

_____

_____

_____

_____

Step 2: Now, take a look at your list. What can you start doing right now? Pick one of the easiest things to organize and do something about it today. If you've always wanted to go camping in the hills, get your travel guide, pick a location, set a date, invite friends, and you're on your way to a great vacation and a happier you!

_____

_____

_____

_____

_____

_____

_____

_____

_____

_____

_____

_____

_____

_____

Now don't stop at the first one! Look back at your list and start scheduling things in. After all, there's no reason why "someday" can't be today.

Making it work

Getting started on your "someday" list will give you a buzz, but if you want to keep buzzing, you have to keep going! Start by:

✦ **Planning ahead.** Make sure that leisure activities don't get squeezed out by work and other commitments. Schedule at least one activity per month. Put it in your diary or calendar and look forward to it!

✦ **Involving others.** One of the keys to happy leisure time is having someone to spend it with. Get others involved in your activities, and you'll not only expand your horizons and learn something new, but you'll also feel great and have a whole lot of fun!

Getting active

Time out for learning new skills, playing sports, or focusing on a challenge is known as active leisure. It's when you're likely to be in "flow"—that feeling of being so engrossed in something that time seems to stand still (as defined by psychologist Mihaly Csikszentmihalyi).

"Flow" is most likely to occur when you've got a challenging goal that requires some skill. It happens when you're concentrating and when you get an immediate response or reward (think about the satisfaction you get when you hit that perfect shot in a tennis match). You have to have a sense of control to be in "flow"; the task has to be manageable but only just—you still have to push yourself. In sum, it can occur when you're doing anything that stops you from thinking about yourself and gets you completely focused on what you're doing. When that happens, you feel fantastic. (Afterward, that is—at the time you're too busy concentrating to notice.) You feel strong, smart, accomplished, motivated, and full of energy. In short, it's when you're at your best!

Some flow-inducing activities: skiing; singing; acting; performing; dancing; programming a computer; reading a great book (usually something that gets you thinking); deep, involved conversation; knitting and needlework; chess; poker; rock climbing; cooking; driving; and writing (people even report being in flow at work).

What have you been doing when you've been in "flow"? How can you organize your time so that you get to experience it more often?

Lifestyle Challenge 2: How can I make the most of every day?

Imagine the luxury of a week's vacation in the most relaxing location you can conjure up. You could be reading a book in a hammock strung between two palm trees, clear blue water lapping the sand nearby. You might be curled up with a glass of red wine by a roaring fire, with music playing in the background and snow-covered mountains visible through the window. You might be hiking your way up the snow-covered mountains, the blistering cold wind piercing your skin, backpack in tow, with the world spread before you as a treacherous yet exhilarating landscape. Whatever turns you on. The important thing is that you're enjoying the simple pleasures that life affords, even if just for a little while.

Pleasure is all about momentary happiness. It's enjoying the sound, sight, taste, and feel of a situation. It doesn't generally last very long, but your sense of well-being peaks when it does. It often happens on vacation, but it's not just the stuff of vacations—it's something you can have every day.

Taking time

Vegging out all day every day may not be good for your long-term happiness, but taking time out to treat yourself to something pleasurable is a great strategy for making the most of life. By taking time out of the daily grind to do something for yourself, you not only feel good and recharge your batteries, but you generally get a better perspective on whatever has been getting you down. Or, if you're feeling really strung out, take a whole day just for yourself and fill it with things that you love doing. It's a great pick-me-up.

"I never take time off work, but recently I was just so stressed out, I felt as though something was going to snap

if I didn't take a break, so I booked myself into a day spa. I had a wonderful massage, spa, and body scrub. Then I went for a long walk by the beach in the afternoon, went home and read a book for a couple of hours, and then had dinner and a couple of drinks with a girlfriend. An early night and a good night's sleep topped it off. By the next day I was ready for whatever life could throw at me." **Karen, 30**

If you want to get the most pleasure out of every day of your life, try these tips.

✦ **Notice the little things.** The perfect parking spot, an e-mail from a friend just saying hi, and the smell of springtime are just some of the simple pleasures in everyday life that can give you a buzz if you take the time to pay attention to them. When something bright pops up during your day, notice it and smile. You'll walk away happier.

✦ **Savour the moment.** When you do get the time to do something enjoyable, make sure you savour it. The best way to do this is to share it with other people. Or you could keep a memento and put it somewhere to remind you (glancing at a postcard from a favorite vacation or a photo of a great time with friends can take you back there in a heartbeat). Pay attention to every sound, taste, touch, and smell, and imprint them on your memory so that you can revisit them later. Most importantly, just get totally immersed in the experience, and don't think about anything at all. Just enjoy it.

✦ **Don't get too much of a good thing.** The challenge when it comes to pleasure (yes, there is one) is finding the right balance between too much and not enough. The joy of a pleasurable experience—whether it's an afternoon in the sun, chocolate ice cream, or your first beer of the evening—is in its novelty. Your brain is wired to notice new sensations much more acutely than those it regularly experiences. You just can't get that feeling back in quite the same way once it has passed (not for a while anyway). So make sure that you space out your treats so that you truly appreciate them.

So far in the book we've talked a lot about thinking and doing. While goals and activity are important, it's easy to let them take over and find yourself treating life as a list of things to check off. You also need time to rest, to be, and to experience life as it happens. Focusing on pleasure is about simply being. Set aside an evening to spend by yourself. Breathe, meditate, savor the smell of bread baking, marvel at a new rose coming into bloom. Slow down and absorb yourself in right now. Taking time and space to be is wonderful for your mind, body, and soul. It can help you feel peaceful and put your worries into perspective. Try it!

Health Hitch 1: My health is starting to worry me. Help!

Have you been bitten by the health bug? Do you get up early, go for a run, and have a nutritious breakfast of juice and cereal? Are you getting plenty of sleep, going to the gym at least three times a week, drinking just the right amount of purified water, taking a range of vitamin supplements, and eating green vegetables? No? Well, you're not alone.

We all have the best intentions when it comes to living a healthy lifestyle, but we all know that it's much easier to eat the wrong things, do minimal exercise, drink too much, and occasionally consume other substances that probably aren't doing much for our health. Getting into healthy habits is hard work and not something we're all that inclined to do, particularly in our 20s.

Turning 30 can be a different proposition. The approach of the big 3-0 can be the jolt you need to start taking your health and fitness more seriously, particularly if, like Vicki, something brings your mortality clearly into view.

"My two aunts on my father's side had breast cancer, and one of them died from it. Back then we were under the impression that because the cancer affected people on my father's side of the family it wouldn't affect me. Then, when I was about 26, they discovered the breast cancer gene and that both of my aunts carried it. At first I didn't want to be tested. I just really didn't want to know. But as I got older it

somehow became more important to find out. I had the blood test and found out that I also carry the gene for breast cancer. The specialist told me that with my family history I should start having regular check-ups when I became ten years younger than my youngest relative to be diagnosed. My youngest aunt was 39 when she was diagnosed. At 29 I was suddenly faced with my own mortality."
Vicki, 31

If you're turning 30 and, for whatever reason, you feel the time has come to treat your body more like a temple and less like a dustbin, the way to do it is to get into good health habits.

A new habit is basically a change in your behavior. You have to change what you're doing now to whatever is more productive. It takes a little while and it takes some discipline, but it's really not that complicated. You can do it!

Making a case for change

Making any change is easier if you know exactly why you're doing it. But often when it comes to your health, you try to make changes just because you feel you "should," rather than because you have a clear picture of the benefits.

Lisa's story

Take Lisa's example. She wanted to take better care of her health by giving up smoking and taking up exercise, but it was something she talked about (constantly) and never did anything about. Then one day she sat down and made her case for change.

Cost of staying the same	Benefits of making the change
✦ I feel lethargic and miserable.	✦ I'll have more energy and feel happier (and proud of myself).
✦ My health is getting worse. I have this hideous cough!	✦ I'm taking control of my health.
✦ I spend too much money on cigarettes.	✦ I'll save money.
✦ My long-term health is at risk.	✦ I'll probably live longer.
✦ I've put on weight sitting in the office all day.	✦ I'll look better.

When Lisa looked at the list, she realized that her case for change was pretty compelling. This was the kick-start she needed, as she could see that some things would improve immediately. She knew that it wouldn't necessarily be an easy challenge to take on, but she could also see the long-term benefits, so she made a start.

The first step is often the most difficult, but it gets easier from then on! Lisa decided to take up running and asked a friend to run with her. Their first morning pounding the pavement was an absolute struggle, but she felt more alive afterward than she had for ages. So they carried on, and to push herself further Lisa set herself a goal of completing a half-marathon by the end of the year. She did some research, found a half-marathon being run not far from her home, signed up for it, and put the entry form up in her bedroom as a bit of added motivation.

Lisa stuck with it. She didn't beat herself up when she didn't feel like running. She just took a break for a day or two and set a target to start again on a specific day. She ran the half-marathon and realized that not only had she achieved her goal, but she had actually gotten into the habit of doing regular exercise. She felt great! As for giving up smoking, that was easy once she'd started running. She knew she just couldn't physically do both! So she not only achieved something she'd been talking about for years, but she also saved money and looked and felt fantastic.

Exercise: Your case for change

Step 1: Write down your case for change below.

Cost of staying the same	Benefits of making the change

Step 2: Take action.

What can you do to improve your diet today? How will you keep it up? (Remember, writing down your goals and looking at them often increases the likelihood of your achieving them.)

_____

_____

_____

_____

_____

_____

_____

_____

_____

What exercise can you do this week? Remember, exercise isn't just about going to the gym. There is so much you can do now, from ju-jitsu or yoga to a brisk walk to the bus stop (instead of taking the car). Find something that appeals to you and find someone to share it with for extra motivation. Good luck!

_____

_____

_____

_____

_____

_____

_____

_____

_____

_____

What's your body up to while you're not looking?

"The other day I saw a magazine cover that said: 'Demi Moore. Age 40. Body of a 29-year-old.' And I thought, 'I'm 29 and I don't have a body anything like that!'" **Charlie, 29**

Oh, the heartache of realizing that you're not in the shape that you were when you were 20—and that you didn't appreciate it enough then! At 30 you're still on the right side of 40 as far as your appearance is concerned, but your body is making subtle adjustments nevertheless. You might have noticed that certain body parts aren't as firm as they once were (cellulite and love handles are here to stay) and that there is the odd crease around your eyes when you smile. Yes, wrinkles! Here's the lowdown on physical changes once you hit 30:

+ Approaching 30 your vision slowly starts to deteriorate, and you might start to lose your high-tone hearing.

+ From your 20s your metabolism decreases at 2 percent per decade. This means you can no longer sustain the burger-and-fries diet of your teens without suffering the consequences.

+ The elasticity and moisture content of your skin peaked in your 20s. It's time to make friends with moisturizer.

+ With each year of sluggish inactivity, you're able to lift 1.5 percent less weight and your aerobic capacity drops up to 1 percent per year.

✦ And in terms of flexibility you're over the hill—for most of us our flexibility peaked when we were 13!

Here's the good news

Don't despair! While you may not be able to do much about fine lines and gray hair (without the assistance of a friendly plastic surgeon and a packet of hair dye), there's evidence to suggest that you can retain almost all of the physical abilities that you had in your 20s if you continue to exercise as frequently and intensely as you did then. The reason we often end up out of shape at 30 is that with other competing priorities physical exercise tends to slip further down the list of things of things to do, and if you don't use it, you lose it! So get out there. Go on!

Health Hitch 2: These Turning 30 Blues are more than just blues.

You probably have a fairly good idea about what you can do to maintain your physical health, but how much thought do you give to your emotional health? If you're feeling particularly low for a long period of time, if you're stressed or anxious, or if you find yourself doing things you'd rather not (overeating, overspending, smoking too much), you might think it's just part and parcel of everyday life, but your emotional health is as important as your physical condition—and just as easy to do something about.

"When I was in my early 20s I didn't take stuff too seriously. I had problems, everyone does. I split up with my first long-term girlfriend and I had trouble finding a full-time job. I just got on with it, though. You just do, don't you? Recently, things have been worse. My problems seem bigger somehow. Harder to overcome. I haven't been sleeping, and I feel kind of out of it a lot of the time. I went to the doctor, and he put me on antidepressants. I'm starting to get on top of things now, and I really need to make sure that I don't end up in that state again." **Max, 33**

Facts:

✦ Roughly one in four people suffer from a diagnosable emotional problem at any given time. These people are not all hanging out together somewhere a long way away from you. They are your friends, your family, your colleagues. They might be you.

✦ Emotional problems include serious illnesses such as schizophrenia and bipolar disorder but also anger, social anxiety and shyness, low self-esteem and self-confidence, grief, stress, panic attacks, worry, addiction, depression, and compulsive behavior. In fact, any behavior or emotional symptom that makes life particularly difficult can be considered an emotional health issue. All the above are pretty common, and you can do something about all of them.

✦ Many people first experience symptoms of emotional problems during their 20s and 30s.

✦ The number of people in their early 30s who report symptoms of depression and anxiety has doubled in the last decade.

Getting help

"I was going through a difficult phase with work, and one day I woke up and knew I couldn't get out of bed and face the world. In all honesty it is the scariest thing that has ever happened to me. Eventually I got myself to a doctor with the help of a friend, and she recommended a therapist. The therapy focused on helping me think more positively about myself and easing off my relentless pursuit of achievement. The psychologist helped me to bring pleasure back into my life, change my way of thinking, and become more assertive. It was a slow process, but I stuck with it and eventually got better." Nick, 32

Nick found out the hard way that pushing yourself to do more and do better can eventually do you in. Maintaining your emotional health is about maintaining balance, a healthy attitude, and a sense of perspective about life and its challenges. Of course, that's not always as easy as it sounds. If you feel that you're not coping or that you could be getting more out of life or feeling better about the world, you must see a physician, psychologist, or counselor. They can help with practical advice about getting back on top of things. (Therapy is not always about lying on a couch, digging deep into your darkest secrets and blaming it all on your mother. It can be a very practical process of discovering what's not working in your life and taking action to change it.)

Ready to take on the world

There are plenty of other practical things that you can do to keep yourself in great emotional condition. In fact, everything we have covered so far in this chapter will help. A good diet, exercise, relaxation, interests, and hobbies are all vital to keeping you on top of life's challenges and feeling great. Other things include:

+ **Hanging out with friends and family.** Make sure you spend time regularly relaxing with the people close to you, and call on them when you're feeling down or stressed out.

+ **Pets.** Research suggests that if you have a pet, you are significantly less likely to be stressed and far more likely to enjoy a happy, healthy life than your non-pet-owning counterparts. Get yourself a goldfish!

+ **Avoiding bad habits.** You know the ones we mean. No matter how good it feels at the time, don't drink too much or dabble in other recreational substances as a means of escaping stress. It just means that you don't develop your own ways of coping.

+ **Setting yourself a routine.** Sounds a bit boring, but if you get up early and exercise or meditate, you'll be much better prepared to cope with the ordeals of the day. Relaxing at the end of the day by reading before bed or taking a hot shower or bath also helps. Make the beginning and the end of your day as peaceful as possible, and you'll sleep better and feel better.

✦ **Growing a garden** (or at least a potted plant.) Caring for a plant and watching it grow and thrive is satisfying and good for the soul.

Making it happen in lifestyle and health

Phew! We've covered a lot in this chapter, and some of it was a bit intense. Your final task is to get up and running with your goals for a healthier and happier lifestyle. Do it now! Get a pen and write your goal and action plan below. Do you want to focus on reorganizing your leisure time, making the most of your everyday life, improving your physical health, revitalizing your emotional health, or all four?

There is no limit to how many changes you can make, but the key is to make sure they are achievable. And if you find your motivation waning, remind yourself of your case for change—why you wanted to get fit or start French classes in the first place.

Most importantly, if you need to talk to someone about an important health issue (physical or emotional), see a physician as soon as possible. He or she can then refer you to an appropriate professional.

Exercise: Taking action in lifestyle and health

Leisure, pleasure, and health goals:

_____

_____

_____

_____

_____

_____

_____

_____

_____

_____

_____

_____

_____

_____

_____

_____

_____

_____

_____

_____

_____

_____

_____

_____

My leisure, pleasure, and health action plan:

1. _____

2. _____

3. _____

4. _____

5. _____

6. _____

7. _____

8. _____

9. _____

10. _____

Action tips for health and lifestyle

✦ **Think solutions.** It's tempting when you're trying to change something in your life to get distracted by all of the problems that come your way. Maybe you've just started your "get fit" campaign when a big project comes up at work. Suddenly your plans to leave work on time to go running in the evenings have gone out the window. Instead of working out, you're going to be stuck in the office eating pizza for dinner! Rather than getting down about it and wallowing in the problem, try thinking about the solution. Given that the situation is what it is, what can you do to continue to make progress toward your goal? Brainstorm as many solutions as you can (even ridiculous ones), then pick the best one and get on with it!

✦ **Celebrate success.** It's important to acknowledge your achievements. By thinking about how you achieved your goal, you learn about what most contributed to your success and you'll be able to use that next time. Also, recognizing your success makes you feel good about yourself! Even more essential is to recognize your achievements along the way and reward yourself for these, too. It's easy to think about the progress you *haven't* made and forget the progress you have. To keep yourself motivated, keep an eye on your small wins and celebrate them.

CHAPTER 7
Staying Happy

Ten reasons why turning 30 is the best thing since sliced bread

1. You can stay in without sounding really boring.

2. You can go on cooking binges and attend evening classes without people thinking you're weird.

3. You can spend your weekends enjoying the delights of home decorating.

4. There is no pressure to fit into small outfits.

5. There is no pressure to be cool.

6. You get along with your parents (better).

7. You don't have to live with ten other people who you don't really like that much.

8. You can listen to music from your teens and say you're into "retro."

9. It's okay to sound like your parents (sometimes).

10. It's okay to simply be yourself.

So you're working your way through your Turning 30 Blues, and you've got yourself a one-way ticket toward an exciting and inspiring 30-something life. You're on the verge of something new and wonderful. Turning 30 is full of new experiences: buying a house, having a child, establishing credit, staying in a job for more than six months. Some of the past will be left behind, but you can take the best of it with you as you move on to the future you really want.

By now you've taken a good look at your life and come up with a way forward in work, love, close relationships, health, and leisure. You know yourself better and have a clear idea of your values, strengths, and personal style, all of which will help you choose wisely from the many options out there and free you from simply following the expectations of others. You have a dream of the future and some goals to move you step-by-step toward that future. What now?

Exercise: Your lessons learned

This book is full of your notes and exercises, and you can refer back to these at any point in your journey. Now is your chance to step back and consider what are the most important things that you have learned so far.

What really sticks in your mind?

What insights have made a lasting impression on you?

What are you excited about?

What do you think will make the biggest difference to your life?

Write your thoughts below. Write them in your diary or stick them onto your mirror so you are reminded of them every day and encouraged to act on them.

My lessons learned

_____

_____

_____

_____

_____

_____

_____

_____

_____

My lessons learned (cont.)

_____
_____
_____
_____
_____
_____
_____
_____
_____
_____
_____
_____
_____
_____
_____
_____
_____
_____
_____
_____
_____
_____
_____

Pizza anyone?

Remember your Pizza of Life from chapter 1? Your scores are a quick indicator of how you're feeling in each area right now. Give yourself a couple of months to start making changes and then go back to your pizza. Score each area again. Are your scores different?

Most people find that their scores increase not only in the area they are particularly focusing on but also in other pizza slices. It seems that the good feelings associated with taking control and making positive changes are contagious!

"I did the pizza in March and all my scores were pretty average. One of my lowest scores was Nearest & Dearest— although I knew a lot of people, I wanted more close friends in my life. So I tried to make changes in this area, and over time I think I learned to be more open to people and made more effort to get to know them. When I redid the pizza in July, my Nearest & Dearest score had shot from a 4 to 7. What I was surprised about was that some other areas had picked up, too, and it seemed that the fact that I was making progress in one area had somehow made the rest seem better, too." **Maria, 33**

Do you truly want to be in a position to boost those Pizza of Life scores and move closer to your Perfect Future? Here are some final thoughts on happiness (and how to find it).

Happiness first

Ups and downs are a normal part of life for every one of us.

All the emotions we feel, both positive and negative, are part of being human. The important thing is to stay strong, accept the lulls, deal with the setbacks, and make the most of the good times.

The good news is that happiness increases as you get older! Research has found that, contrary to what we might expect, as we age we do become happier. Maybe as we get older we just get better at living and learn to do more of the things that make us happy and let go of those that don't.

So there's something to look forward to, but in the meantime, to keep your happiness on track, why not get into these quick happiness habits:

✦ **Wonderful times.** Think back to a great experience that you shared with someone. Reminisce about it with that person, remember the sights, sounds, and feelings. Look through any photos you have. Bring back the moment.

✦ **Count your blessings.** How often do you go to bed worrying about what went wrong today and what will happen tomorrow? Count your blessings instead. Write down three things that went well during the day and why. Think of them as you go to sleep. Then in the morning, instead of dragging yourself out of bed and moping at the prospect of work, think about how many things you have to look forward to that day. Have a competition with yourself, and try to beat the previous day's score.

✦ **Favorite things.** List all of your favorite things. These could be anything from chocolate cake to Manolo

Blahnik shoes to adventure sports. When did you last experience them? Make time for one thing that delights you, however small, every day.

+ **Playtime.** Take a day off in the middle of the week just to play. Yes, you're allowed! Even better, do it with someone you love being with.

+ **Avoid tunnel vision.** Have you ever caught yourself saying, "I'll be happy when I . . . get married, work for myself, lie in the sun, learn to fly, etc.," Do you place all your hopes for a happy life on the achievements of one thing? Does it pan out that way? Often we put happiness on hold until we reach a particular point in our lives and find that our problems don't miraculously disappear when we get there. Although goals are important for moving forward, don't wait to be happy until you achieve them. Make a conscious choice to enjoy the process.

+ **Don't make life a soap opera.** Cut the melodrama by realizing you have a choice in the way you respond to life. Try not to make problems bigger than they are by moaning about how awful your situation is. Do something about it instead.

+ **Take credit.** When good things happen, recognize your contribution. If you catch yourself thinking that getting promoted was all about luck and circumstance, think again. Acknowledge that you got promoted because you're amazing at what you do!

+ **Say thanks.** Acknowledge the most important people in

your life—friends who have got you through tough times, parents who are always there, partners who love you even when you're in a bad mood, people at school, college, and work you've learned from, people around and about who are kind and make time for you.

✦ **Ditch your baggage.** By the time we've reached 30, we've often built up enough baggage to last a lifetime and can think of endless reasons to be miserable. Maybe you were dumped by Chris Vaughan, when you were 13, or your parents divorced when you were five, or you didn't take the opportunity to travel when you should have. Whether you were let down by others or by yourself, try to forgive and move on for your own peace of mind. It's not always easy, but it will be worth the effort.

✦ **Stay optimistic.** Optimists are healthier, happier, and more successful. When bad things happen, look for temporary and specific explanations: "I didn't get that particular job because I wasn't feeling on form during the interview that day." But when the good times roll, the opposite applies. Time to think in permanent and global terms: "I got the job because I'm competent, experienced and persuasive."

✦ **Use your strengths.** Remember the strengths you noted in chapter 2? Do more of the things you're good at, and spend less time trying to correct your imperfections. Stretch and challenge yourself in your areas of strength. It will pay off.

Exercise: New perspectives

Taking perspective in life is important. So far you've looked at your post-30 future. Try taking that even further with the following exercise:

Imagine it's your 80th birthday. You are celebrating with family and friends. Take time to review your life. What have you achieved? What do you feel proud of? What is it about you that people value? What are the most significant things that you are celebrating? Write your thoughts below.

_____

_____

_____

_____

_____

_____

_____

_____

_____

_____

_____

_____

_____

_____

_____

_____

_____

_____

_____

_____

_____

_____

_____

_____

_____

_____

_____

_____

_____

The 80th birthday exercise isn't easy to do, but any thoughts will help you get a better perspective on where you are today. Remember, the big 3-0 is young! You've a lifetime ahead of you. The things that you might find yourself worrying about now, like the presentation for Monday morning or the broken light in the bathroom, aren't likely to matter much at the end of the day. At the heart of Buddhist teaching is the eternal question "Did you learn to live well?" What is "living well" to you?

In his theory of happiness, Professor Martin Seligman says that true happiness is associated with a sense of meaning, a sense of contributing to something wider than just yourself, whether this is a relationship, family, community, or society. What brings meaning to your life?

The insights that you've picked up from working through the exercises in this book will help you to answer these questions. Keep them at the back of your mind, and every now and again ask yourself, "Am I living well? What brings meaning to my life?" They are questions you can keep asking yourself for the rest of your days. The answers will change, but the questions will keep you on track for a happy life.

The only thing left to say is good luck for the future. Believe in yourself and enjoy every step of the adventure!

CHAPTER 8
Further Case Studies

Kate's story

Kate, 28 had been working as a financial controller for a marketing company for a few years. She was generally happy with life, but over the past year or so her job had started to get her down. She knew it was time for a career shake-up as her Pizza of Life score confirmed.

Kate's Pizza of Life looks like this:

| Earning a living 4/10 | Love life 7/10 |
| Nearest & dearest 9/10 | Health & lifestyle 6/10 |

Earning a living: I'm so bored! I've had enough of finance, but what do I do instead? I feel like I have grown out of this job, but the future is just a black hole.

Love life: Going well on the whole. I've been with Mark for three years now, and it's going strong. Would it be better if we saw more of each other, though? We spend far too much time in the office and not enough time together.

Nearest and dearest: My family is always supportive, and my friends are great. It's great when we get together. Again my only complaint would be that I don't see them as often as I'd like to.

Health and lifestyle: Not bad. I'm not unfit, and I get to the gym on a regular-ish basis. Would like to have some sort of interest that I could take up.

In Kate's Perfect Future letter, she wrote the following:

Dear Kate,

How are you doing? I can't wait to update you on all that's been going on over the last couple of years!

Mark and I have moved in together—it seemed like a big step at the time, but now I can't see what all the fuss was about. It feels like we've got a home together, and I love the sense of security around our relationship.

The most exciting development is my new career! You wouldn't believe what I ended up doing; it's so different from my old finance jobs. I've started a well-being studio with my friend Jackie. It's a fantastic place, really calming and beautiful; I love just being in that space. People come to relax and chill out, and there are loads of different treatments and activities on offer like

Pilates, massages, and acupuncture. It's been hard work getting to where we are now, and so different from my past jobs, but I'm so pleased that I was brave enough to take charge of my career and do something like this! I feel proud of what I do and what I've achieved, and I love talking to people about it.

I suppose I have the well-being studio to thank for my improved fitness—one of the perks of the job is free classes, and I've been making the most of them. I'm a complete yoga fanatic. I've also recently taken up painting—which I haven't done since I was at school. I'm not that great but really enjoy it. My friends are less impressed when I hand out my "artwork" as birthday presents!

My friends and family are really well, and now that the hard work is over with the well-being studio, I get to see them so much more. One of my best friends met a Spanish guy and has moved to Spain, and I'm planning a trip over to visit them in the summer.

With lots of love,

Kate

Kate's career goals

From her letter, Kate knew she was ready for something else in her career, but what would be the right move? Her career story was a familiar one in the run up to 30. She'd been a bright student and had many options to choose from. Influenced by her father, she chose to study accounting like him and ended up moving from one "good job" in finance to the next. Until now she hadn't given much thought to what she really wanted to do; she'd just done the things expected of her. To change all that, she set herself a career goal: to explore her career direction and reach four or five career options for the future.

Values, strengths, and personal style

This is what Kate came up with when she examined her values, strengths, and personal style:

Values	Strengths	Personal style
Independence	Influencing	Sociable
Helping others	Organizing	Caring
Variety	Entertaining	Confident
Beauty	Motivating others	Decisive

Piecing together the career jigsaw

Step 1: Your dream jobs

1. Well-being studio (as in the "Perfect Future" letter)

2. Restaurateur (love the idea of doing this, I could be the new Wolfgang Puck!)

3. Florist (being surrounded by the beauty of flowers would be wonderful—Don't you have to get up early, though?)

4. Massage therapist (think this would be a relaxing and rewarding job, helping to reduce people's stress and anxieties)

When looking at her ideal jobs and her values, strengths, and personal style, Kate was struck by the strong emphasis on people and relationships. It seemed that a job that involved interacting with people more would suit her (unlike her financial roles).

Step 2: Your skills and knowledge

1. Managing a team

2. Organization (mostly from my social life)

3. Getting along with people

4. Making changes happen

Step 3: Likes and dislikes

Likes	Dislikes
1. Control over own work	1. Politics
2. Working in a team	2. Too much direction
3. Implementing ideas	3. Detailed work
4. Being busy	4. Routine
5. Working on several projects at once	5. Working alone too much

Step 4: Who, what, when, where, and how
Kate reflected on her ideal working experience:

People: Like-minded people who are friends more than colleagues

Environment: Relaxed, friendly, office, studio, or shop

Working practices: Don't mind working unconventional hours, self-employment could be a possibility (if I muster up the courage)

Money: Probably would be okay on a bit less than I earn now

Step 5: Putting the pieces together

Kate then spent time thinking about what she'd learned about herself and was encouraged by her insights. She had a clearer idea of what was behind her dissatisfaction with her current career path and the sort of experience she was looking for next. Through discussions with friends and contacts and further research she came up with some career options that she was interested in finding out more about:

✦ Conference organizer/event manager

✦ Sales manager

✦ Small business manager of some kind (ideally in the well-being/health/beauty field)

✦ Management consultant

Although apprehensive about making changes, Kate's confidence and conviction around her career had increased. Her Pizza of Life score for Earning a Living went from a 4 to a 6!

"I started off completely clueless about why I wasn't happy and what I could do about it, and now I feel like I've got a sense of the future and it's exciting. The thought of doing

something different does scare me, but I know I can't leave things as they are. I just plan to take things slowly and make changes in my own time. It doesn't even matter if I change my mind from one thing to the next at this stage, at least I've taken control. One of the things I would like to do is events management, and I know there are people who do that in my company. I might start by seeing if I can help them out, and get an idea of what it's all about."

Claire's story

Claire, 32, found herself wanting to make some changes in her life. "I'm going through a time when I feel like I want to sort my life out. I'm tired of just drifting along and putting up with stuff that doesn't work for me."

Claire's Pizza of Life looks like this:

Earning a living: The company I work for used to be great, and I loved being part of it. With the recent merger it has become a completely different place, and I'm not sure I want to stay there much longer. Maybe it's time my aerobics became more than a hobby?

Love life: Been single for quite a while, and I've loved the freedom and independence. Met someone quite recently, though, and I'm enjoying spending time with him, so we'll have to see what happens.

Nearest and dearest: This is a mixed bag. On the plus side, I get along well with my parents and see them about once a month. When it comes to friends, things aren't so good. I've moved around quite a bit in my 20s and had a couple of disastrous relationships. Because of this, I've lost touch with friends from the past, and I'd like some good friends in my life now. The problem is that I've got no idea how to achieve that. I know people, but my relationships with them stop at a certain level, and I seem to lack the confidence to develop friendships.

Health and lifestyle: I'm an aerobics junkie and go to the gym three times a week, so generally I'm in good shape. I'm also good at making time for myself. Have a long-standing ambition to sing but am pretty scared about that so keep putting it off!

By doing the Pizza of Life, Claire managed to pinpoint the things she wanted to change: "I found the pizza so helpful, as I kind of got an overview of my life and discovered the specific areas where things weren't working. I also realized that a lot was going well in my life." Claire's areas for attention were career and friends. She had some ideas about how to improve her work life and had already enrolled in a course to become an aerobics instructor, but was stuck when it came to friends.

In Claire's Perfect Future letter, she wrote the following:

Dear Claire,

So much has happened since we last spoke. Life is wonderful. Where to begin?

I finally quit my job! I finally realized all the years worrying about letting them down by leaving were wasted on them. They are a big company now, and they certainly didn't spend any time worrying about my happiness, progression, or whether I'd stay or not, so I don't know why I spent all that time worrying about it! Of course it was rather scary leaving behind the security of a regular paid job, but I spent the last year while I was there taking courses for my new career, which I shall tell you about next! It was hugely emotional leaving all the people I'd worked with for years, but so many had already left.

Anyway! Let me tell you about what I do now! I spent the last year training in fitness and sports injury, and I now work as an aerobics instructor, a personal trainer, and I also accept physician referrals for exercise programs. I get referrals from local doctors and the satisfaction of seeing my clients progress is just wonderful. One of my clients bought me a lovely flower arrangement the other day to say thank you. I was so touched! It was a struggle to cope financially, but I kept a close eye on finances. I also have a part-time job working in a local shop, which is going well. I really enjoy ordering in new stock and advising people on their purchases.

My best friend came over the other day to drag me out for some window shopping and gossip. I don't know what I would have done without her. She's encouraged me so much over the last year and listened to me moaning! We've had some fantastic girly days out in the past year. Things are also going well with John— he took me out for a romantic dinner last week to celebrate our year anniversary. So much has happened!

Biggest shock—I've got a part singing in a stage show! Looks like all those singing lessons paid off. I'm also doing a dance number, which I am really looking forward to. I hope someone videos the performance; I've not been on stage since I was at school.

Anyway, I must go. I'm going to the movies with John tonight, and then tomorrow I'm helping my best friend decorate her new apartment.

Much love,

Claire

Claire's plans

Nearest & dearest goals: To improve the friendships in my life so I have one or two people I can talk to about stuff that's important to me, have fun with, and trust.

My nearest & dearest action plan:

1. Fight my fears and join singing class! It will be a great way to meet new people

2. Offer to help Jane at work to prepare for her exams

3. Go over to Sue's house and take her a bunch of flowers for her birthday

4. Suggest going for a quick drink after aerobics with a couple of the girls

By taking these actions, Claire upped her focus on friendship. When looking at her values, strengths, and personal style Claire found there was a strong relationship theme that ran through them all. This confirmed that close relationships were important to her, and she was encouraged to do something about them. She also realized that she was someone who needed her own space, so it was often tempting to make less of an effort with people in order to do that. She'd ended up spending too much time by herself, and what she really needed was a healthy balance.

Claire started making more of an effort with the people she met. Instead of keeping to herself, she organized get-togethers and offered her help to others. *"I would typically think of doing things like going over to see someone, or suggesting we get together, but stop myself for fear of seeming too pushy or sad or annoying. I started to push my fears aside and do those things, and found that mostly people responded really well."*

When Claire re-did her Pizza of Life four months later, her Nearest & Dearest score boosted from 5 to 8. With some clear direction, courage, and dedicated effort she managed to make some positive changes toward her ideal future.

RESOURCES

General/lifestyle/health

Allen Carr's *Easy Way to Stop Smoking*, Penguin Books, 1988.

Mihaly Csikszentmihalyi, *Living Well: The Psychology of Everyday Life*, Weidenfeld & Nicolson, 1997.

The Mind Gym: Wake Your Mind Up, Time Warner, 2005.

Anthony H. Grant and Jane Greene, *Coach Yourself: Make Real Change in Your Life*, Momentum, 2001.

Karen Reivich and Andrew Shatte, *The Resilience Factor: 7 Keys to Finding Your Inner Strength and Overcoming Life's Hurdles*, Broadway Books, 2003.

Barry Schwartz, *The Paradox of Choice: Why More Is Less*, HarperCollins, 2004.

Martin E. P. Seligman, *Authentic Happiness*, Simon & Schuster, 2002.

Career

Laurence G. Boldt, *Zen and the Art of Making a Living: A Practical Guide to Creative Career Design*, Penguin Books, 1999.

Richard Nelson Bolles, *What Color Is Your Parachute?*, Ten Speed Press, 1981.

Susan Jeffers, *Feel the Fear and Do It Anyway*, Century, 1988.

John Lees, *How to Get a Job You'll Love: A Practical Guide to Unlocking Your Talents and Finding Your Ideal Career*, McGraw-Hill Education, 2004.

Barbara Sher and Barbara Smith, *I Could Do Anything If I Only Knew What It Was: How to Discover What You Really Want and How to Get It*, Dell, 1995.

Love/Nearest & Dearest

Mary Balfour, *Smart Dating: How to Find Your Man*, Element Books, 2004.

John Gottman and Nan Silver, *The Seven Principles for Making Marriage Work*, Crown Publications, 1999.

Douglas Stone, Bruce Patton and Sheila Heen, *Difficult Conversations: How to Discuss What Matters Most*, Penguin Books, 1999.

INDEX